JOURNAL OF LAW
&
CYBER WARFARE

FOREWORD
Cyber Warfare, What are the Rules?
By Daniel B. Garrie

ARTICLES
Cyber Attacks and the Laws of War
By Michael Gervais

If You Wish Cyber Peace, Prepare for Cyber War: The Need
for the Federal Government to Protect Critical Infrastructure
From Cyber Warfare.
By Michael Preciado

They Did it For the Lulz: Future Policy Considerations in the
Wake of Lulz Security and Other Hacker Groups' Attacks on
Stored Private Customer Data
By Jesse Noa

A New Perspective on the Achievement of Psychological
Effects from Cyber Warfare Payloads: The Analogy of
Parasitic Manipulation of Host Behavior
By Dr. Mils Hills

Volume 1 | Winter 2012 | Issue 1
(c) 2012 – 2013. Journal of Law & Cyber Warfare.
All Rights Reserved.

www.jlcw.org

Cyber Attacks and the Laws of War*

By Michael Gervais**

I. INTRODUCTION

In 1949, John Von Neumann—a mathematician and an early architect of computing systems—presented at the University of Illinois a series of lectures called the *Theory and Organization of Complicated Automata*, where he explored the possibility of developing machines that self-replicate.[1] Von Neumann envisioned machines that could build self-copies and pass on their programming to their progeny. While his ideas had legitimate applications, such as large-scale mining, many observers also consider it to be the theoretical precursor to the modern-day computer virus.[2] Self-replication is a defining characteristic of computer viruses and worms. Through self-replication, computer code populates computer systems exponentially. Computer viruses and worms have the capacity for constructive applications,

* A version of this article appeared in the Berkeley Journal of International Law. Michael Gervais, *Cyber Attacks and the Laws of War*, 30 Berkeley J. Int'l L. 525 (2012). It has been modified and reprinted here with the express permission of the Berkeley Journal of International Law.

** Michael Gervais graduated in 2011 from Yale Law School, where he served as senior editor of the Yale Journal of International Law (YJIL). Before law school, Michael Gervais spent time serving as an AmeriCorps* VISTA and as a Jesse M. Unruh Assembly Fellow in the California State Legislature.

[1.] *When Did the Term 'Computer Virus' Arise?*, SCI. AM. (Oct. 19, 2001), http://www.scientificamerican.com/article.cfm?id=when-did-the-term-compute.

[2] *Id.*

but they are most often malware—malicious software that is hostile, intrusive, and unwelcome.[3]

The first generation of malware in the 1970s was mostly experimental and did little damage beyond using computer memory and annoying its victims. When personal computing took hold in the 1980s, malware evolved into something more destructive. Viruses, worms, and other forms of malware spread quickly throughout the Internet, destroying data, overloading systems, and generally causing havoc.[4] The Advanced Research Projects Agency (ARPA)—a research wing of the US Department of Defense (now known as DARPA)[5]—responded by funding a Computer Emergency Response Team at Carnegie Mellon University to coordinate and respond to computer security issues.[6] Additionally, ARPA asked the National Research Council (NRC) to study the "security and trustworthiness" of American computing and communications systems. In 1991, the NRC issued its report. Presciently, the report noted that "[t]omorrow's

---

[3] *Malware*, OXFORD ENGLISH DICTIONARY ONLINE, http://www.oed.com/view/Entry/267413?redirectedFrom=malware#e id (last visited Mar. 1, 2012).

[4] *The History Of Computer Viruses*, VIRUS-SCAN-SOFTWARE.COM, http://www.virus-scan-software.com/virus-scan-help/answers/the-history-of-computer-viruses.shtml (last visited Mar. 2, 2011); *see also Morris Worm*, TECHOPEDIA, http://www.techopedia.com/definition/27371/morris-worm (last visited Mar. 1, 2012).

[5] DARPA and ARPA are used interchangeably because the agency recently switched its name from the Advanced Research Projects Agency (ARPA) to the Defense Advanced Research Projects Agency (DARPA).

[6] *Meet CERT*, SOFTWARE ENG'G INST., CARNEGIE MELLON UNIV., http://www.cert.org/meet_cert/#bkgd (last visited Feb. 5, 2012).

terrorist may be able to do more damage with a keyboard than with a bomb."[7]

It has been over twenty years since the NRC highlighted the risks to computer systems. Since then, the global community has grown more reliant upon the everyday use of computers and the Internet. The ever-increasing interdependence of computer networks has sparked a parallel growth in the complexity of cyber attacks. As computer systems have evolved, so have the attacks. Infrastructure, the financial system, commerce, government operations, including the military and, ultimately, national security have gone online, leaving the "security and trustworthiness" of the computing and communications system's increasingly vulnerable to hostile actors. With each new cyber attack, nation-states are seeing the potential vulnerabilities—as well as opportunities—of an interconnected society.[8] Cyberspace has become a new battleground for warfare.

The lawfulness of cyber warfare remains unsettled. The international community designed the international instruments that form the laws of war in response to kinetic technologies. As warfare evolves with new technologies, our understanding of how to interpret these international instruments changes as well, leaving decision makers uncertain as to how to apply the laws of war to cyber attacks. This is a troubling scenario because recent events confirm that cyber warfare is operational. Although still in its infancy, the capabilities of cyber attacks are innumerable. This article examines the capabilities of a cyber attack and the relationship between cyber attacks and the existing international instruments that govern the laws of war.

---

[7] Sys. Sec. Study Comm., Nat'l Research Council, Computers at Risk: Safe Computing in the Information Age (1991).

[8] Marco Roscini, *World Wide Warfare—Jus Ad Bellum and the Use of Cyber Force*, 14 MAX PLANCK U.N.Y.B. 85, 97-98 (2010).

Part I discusses the architecture of cyberspace and how it operates. Part II examines the framework of international humanitarian law and its application to cyber warfare. Ultimately, I contend, the international instruments in place do not answer all the relevant questions that cyber attacks generate. Indeed, they cannot even answer all the questions surrounding the forms of warfare that they were created to govern. However, these international instruments are helpful in determining how cyber attacks ought to be understood under the existing *jus ad bellum* (use of war) and *jus in bello* (wartime conduct) frameworks.

A. SHORT HISTORY OF CYBERSPACE AND ITS ARCHITECTURE

The Internet is a by-product of the science and technology race of the Cold War. After World War II, tension quickly escalated between the United States and the Soviet Union. The Soviet Union's launch of the Sputnik satellite in 1957 caused particular alarm in the United States.[9] The launch changed world perception of the United States as a technological superpower, creating a sense of vulnerability among the American people, and elevating the international status of the Soviet Union.

With the threat of nuclear war looming over the nation, the US government responded to the perceived gap with a shift in strategy that emphasized technology and science.[10] The federal government poured money into science, engineering, mathematics education and research at all levels. Among its many initiatives, the

---

[9] *Videos of 50 Years of DARPA Achievements, The Formative Years: 1958–1975,* DARPA, http://www.darpa.mil/VideoFiles/01_The_Formative_Years_1958_-_1975_200807171333371.wmv (last visited Feb. 5, 2013).0

[10] Larry Abramson, *Sputnik Left Legacy for U.S. Science Education,* NPR (Sept. 30, 2007), http://www.npr.org/templates/story/story.php?storyId=14829195.

United States created and funded the Advanced Research Projects Agency (ARPA) within the Department of Defense a few months after the launch of Sputnik. Its task was to maintain the technological superiority of the US military and prevent "technological surprise." It would prove invaluable for the creation of the Internet.[11]

One concern for the military was the theoretical ability of a Soviet nuclear strike to disable completely American communications systems. The prevailing view was that the command and control structure of the US government and military could not withstand such an attack. Therefore, military analysts saw a robust communications network that would survive an attack as a necessity in any nuclear confrontation.[12]

The critical component of survivability was a technique called "distributed communications." Under conventional communication systems, such as telephone networks, switching, i.e., the process of channeling data from input to output ports, was concentrated and hierarchical.[13] Thus, a call went to a local office, then to a regional or national switching office if a user needed a connection beyond the local area.[14] Under this system, if a local office were destroyed, many users would be cut off. Responding to this communications threat, Paul Baran, a researcher at the Air Force's think tank, the Rand Corporation, conceived of a distributed system composed of multiple switching nodes with many attached links.[15] Under Baran's system, if one node failed, the information would simply take an alternative route. This redundancy made cutting off service to users

---

[11] *Creating & Preventing Strategic Surprise*, DARPA, http://www.darpa.mil (last visited Feb. 5, 2012).

[12] *See* Videos of 50 Years of DARPA Achievements, The Formative Years: 1958–1975, supra note 9.

[13] Janet Abbate, Inventing the Internet 11 (2000).

[14] *Id.*

[15] *Id.*

more difficult.[16] Moreover, Baran proposed locating the nodes far from population centers to make the system more secure.[17]

Most importantly, Baran created a technique of switching to move data through the network as packets—a series of binary numbers ("bits").[18] This innovation proved vital for several reasons: (1) fixed-size packets simplified the design of switching nodes, (2) breaking messages into bits of information made it harder for spies to eavesdrop on communications, and (3) the system was more efficient and flexible for sharing a data link.[19] Although packet switching was inherently more complex because packets of information had to be reassembled for the user, researchers made the system for data transmission less costly to build.[20] Reducing the costs of the system made it more feasible to create a highly redundant and therefore survivable communications system.[21]

Meanwhile, ARPA hired J.C.R. Licklider to head the Information Processing Techniques Office (IPTO).[22] Before joining IPTO, Licklider had imagined a nationwide network of "thinking centers," with responsive, real-time computers.[23] This vision underlay the ARPANET—the precursor to the Internet. As head of the IPTO, Licklider funded technology that put his ideas into practice. In addition, he warned that the dozen or so independent projects would produce incompatible

---

[16] *Id.*

[17] *Id.*

[18] *Id.* at 17–18.

[19] *Id.* at 19.

[20] *Id.* at 20.

[21] *Id.*

[22] *See* Mitch Waldrop, *DARPA and the Internet Revolution, in* DARPA: 50 YEARS OF BRIDGING THE GAP 78, 78 (2008), http://www.darpa.mil/WorkArea/DownloadAsset.aspx?id=2554.

[23] *Id.* at 79.

machines, incompatible computer languages, and incompatible software.[24] However, it was not until the third IPTO director—Robert Taylor—that IPTO organized the fledgling projects around the country around a common vision. Rather than ARPA funding dozens of independent projects, Taylor decided that it was necessary for the remote projects to share computing resources.[25] It was time to build a "network of networks."

To create the ARPA network, researchers made several critical technical decisions that defined its architecture and that of its successor, the Internet. These decisions have ongoing implications for cyber attacks.

First, because there was insufficient funding for ARPA to build its own wires across the country, the government had to move its data through the *civilian* infrastructure already in place—the AT&T telephone system.[26] Second, the government utilized Baran's packet-switching concept. Thus, digital messages were broken into segments of fixed lengths rather than sent through the network continuously.[27] This feature protected against static and distortion by isolating errors and giving the system a chance to fix them. Third, the ARPA network was decentralized.[28] Adhering to Baran's concept of a survivable communications system, rather than engage a master computer to sort and route the packets, each ARPA site read the digital address on the packet as it came in. The site then accepted the packet if the address was local or sent it in the right direction.[29] Finally, instead of asking each site to run packets

---

[24] *Id.* at 79–80.
[25] James Gillies & Robert Cailliau, How the Web Was Born: The Story of the World Wide Web 16 (2000).
[26] Waldrop, *supra* note 22, at 80.
[27] *Id.*
[28] *Id.* at 81.
[29] *Id.*

through its main computers, researchers built Interface Message Processors (IMPs)—the precursor to the modern router—that handled all the routing chores.[30] By using IMPs to handle routing, the main computers on the network had to learn only the IMP's language rather than the language of each computer on the network.[31]

The next challenge was figuring out how to make all of the computers to work together. Because ARPANET linked together many one-of-a-kind machines,[32] it was necessary for the various computers to adopt a standard universal protocol.[33] By 1974, Robert Kahn and Vinton Cerf designed the standard protocol that is still in place today—the Transmission Control Protocol/Internet Protocol (TCP/IP).[34] TCP/IP specifies how data should be formatted, addressed, transmitted, routed, and received at the destination. Over the next few years, Kahn and Cerf developed several operational versions of the protocol and, by 1982, the TCP/IP was reliable enough for the Department of Defense to make it the standard for military computer networking.[35] Finally, in 1983, ARPANET switched over to TCP/IP—and the Internet was born.[36]

Each of these decisions was critical to the formation of the modern-day Internet, but they also created a greater number of targets for cyber attacks. Furthermore, the decision to intertwine the civilian and military infrastructure made it difficult to determine which targets are valid under the law of armed conflict. Despite such consequences, these decisions clearly facilitated communication between computers.

---

[30] *Id.*

[31] *Id.* at 84.

[32] ABBATE, *supra* note 13, at 48.

[33] *See* Waldrop, *supra* note 22, at 84.

[34] *Id.* at 85.

[35] *Id.*

[36] *Id.*

Once the fundamental architecture was in place, the private sector and researchers across the nation collaborated and improved upon others' ideas to build applications that popularized the Internet for mass consumption. These applications included E-mail, the World Wide Web,[37] file transferring, and a host of other programs connecting users to what is known as "cyberspace."[38] Moreover, with the advent of personal computers and Internet Service Providers (ISPs), which linked users to the Internet through the public domain, other networks began to connect to one another, which eventually made ARPANET obsolete.[39]

Thus, over a period of thirty years, the initial problem of how to design a survivable system of communication yielded a tool that forever changed how people communicate. But the growing integration of computers into individuals' lives also made the vulnerabilities of cyberspace increasingly apparent. The entire Internet is shared between civilian and military uses, and between the United States and its adversaries. This level of interconnectedness may be the Internet's greatest virtue—expanding the number of users and creating a global marketplace of ideas—but it also presents a grave security risk.

The largest threats in cyberspace are not accidental. Rather, bad actors design malware to access a computer system without the owner's informed consent. Malware—similar to software—consists of programs or protocols that tell computers what to do. Those instructions are often destructive, intrusive, or annoying.

---

[37] Tim Berners-Lee, a computer programmer at CERN, developed the World Wide Web as a simpler way to provide access to research materials.

[38] *Cyberspace*, OXFORD ENGLISH DICTIONARY ONLINE, http://oed.com/view/Entry/240849?redirectedFrom=cyber%20space#eid (last visited Mar. 1, 2012).

[39] Waldrop, *supra* note 22, at 85.

Unfortunately, just as software has become more innovative and sophisticated over time, so, too, has malware. What began with initial users testing a computer system's capabilities by exploiting its vulnerabilities[40] has escalated into the use of malware to commit cyber crimes. As personal computing and the Internet have grown, the number and impact of bad actors has dramatically increased.

The first versions of malware appeared on the ARPANET as experimental self-replicating programs.[41] Designed to annoy or harass users, these programs usually were harmless, boastful programming challenges or pranks between anonymous users. For example, the first computer virus—the Creeper Virus—simply displayed the message, "I'm the Creeper: Catch me if you can!"[42] Shortly after its release, the Reaper—the first antivirus program—removed the Creeper Virus.[43] In 1988, however, the Morris Worm demonstrated the potential for widespread harm by infecting ten percent of computers connected to the Internet.[44] It was not long before states began using malware as a method of attacking adversaries in what is now known as a cyber attack.

B.   WHAT IS CYBER WARFARE?

---

[40] Thomas M. Chen & Jean-Marc Robert, *The Evolution of Viruses and Worms*, STATISTICAL METHODS IN COMPUTER SECURITY 265, 268 (Thomas M. Chen ed., 2005).

[41] *Id.*

[42] Joseph L. Flatley, Creeper the First Computer Virus Is 40 Years Young Today, ENGADGET (Mar. 17, 2011), http://www.engadget.com/2011/03/17/creeper-the-first-computer-virus-is-40-years-young-today/.

[43] *Id.*

[44] Brian Krebs, *A Short History of Computer Viruses and Attacks*, WASH. POST (Feb. 14, 2003), http://www.washingtonpost.com/ac2/wp-dyn/A50636-2002Jun26 (last visited Mar. 1, 2012); *Morris Worm, supra* note 4.

As developed nations become reliant upon computer systems in every sector of society, opportunities increasingly arise for adversaries to strike inexpensively, remotely, and effectively with little risk. For that reason, states and non-state actors turn to cyberspace to conduct warfare with greater frequency. This Section explores cyber warfare's theater of conflict as well as the definition of a cyber attack in relation to cyber warfare, cybercrime, and other hostile actions taken online.

1.   CYBER WAR'S "THEATER OF CONFLICT"

An integral aspect of evaluating cyber warfare's legal status is determining the active "theater of conflict." If an attack occurs within the active theater of conflict, the law of armed conflict governs. But when a conventional attack occurs outside of the geographically limited theater of conflict, it is less clear how the laws of war apply.[45]

The challenge in defining the theater of conflict in cyber space is that any particular operation will instantaneously cross components of the Internet infrastructure, which is spread throughout multiple countries. Thus, defining the theater of conflict is not as simple as equating cyberspace infrastructure to other forms of civilian or military infrastructure.[46] Fortunately, neither law nor custom supports confining a conflict to geographical boundaries. Such a constraint becomes dangerously illogical in conflicts that inherently cross borders.

---

[45] Job C. Henning, *Embracing the Drone*, N.Y. TIMES, Feb. 20, 2012, http://www.nytimes.com/2012/02/21/opinion/embracing-the-drone.html?pagewanted=all.

[46] *See, e.g.,* Protocol Additional to the Geneva Conventions of 12 August 1949, and Relating to the Protection of Victims of International Armed Conflicts (Protocol I) art. 48, June 8, 1977, 1125 U.N.T.S. 3 [hereinafter Protocol I].

Cyber warfare also allows combatants to fight from extreme distances, which raises a number of ethical and moral considerations. Not unlike the concerns raised in relation to those operating Predator drones,[47] cyber attackers are far from the battlefield. Being removed from the horrors of war, cyber attackers risk becoming emotionally detached from the effects of their attacks, increasing the possibility of unnecessary harm, suffering and collateral damage.

However, while such ethical and moral considerations warrant exploration, the laws of war do not present additional restraints in this respect. For example, international law does not differentiate between hand-to-hand combat and an intercontinental ballistic missile. Similarly, cyberspace should be treated like any other theater of conflict regardless of its expanse or the location of those participating in cyber attacks.

2.   DEFINING CYBER WARFARE

The all-encompassing term "cyber war" is not an apt description for hostile actions in cyberspace because of the wide range of possible intended effects of an attack. It is helpful to be more specific by distinguishing between cyber attacks and cyber exploitation.

The only international agreement that approaches a definition for cyber attacks is the Council of Europe's Convention on Cybercrime—a multilateral treaty that increased cooperation among signatories to combat cyber crimes such as fraud, child pornography,

---

[47] Similar arguments have been made about the "playstation mentality" of drone warfare. *See, e.g.,* Philip Alston, Report of the Special Rapporteur on Extrajudicial, Summary or Arbitrary Executions,   25   (2010), http://www2.ohchr.org/english/bodies/hrcouncil/docs/14session/A.H RC.14.24.Add6.pdf.

and copyright infringement.[48] Because the Convention has not been widely adopted, it is not binding as customary international law.[49] But the Convention demonstrates that international concern exists regarding the use of cyber attacks, and it recognizes a state's duty to prevent these attacks. The treaty aims to harmonize the domestic criminal laws of the signatory states, including adoption of appropriate legislation to criminalize the enumerated cyber offenses. Most relevant for cyber attacks are the Convention's provisions on data and system interference. The Convention requires signatories to adopt laws that criminalize "the damaging, deletion, deterioration, alteration or suppression of computer data without right,"[50] as well as "the serious hindering without right of the functioning of a computer system" by similar means.[51] While the Convention falls short of regulating cyber attacks, its incipient efforts at defining cyber attacks at an international level is significant.

The Department of Defense has not yet defined cyber warfare.[52] But one workable definition of a cyber attack offered by the US Army's *DCSINT Handbook No. 1.02* is: "The premeditated use of disruptive activities, or the threat thereof, against computers and/or networks, with the intention to cause harm or to further social, ideological, religious, political or similar objectives. Or

---

[48] Council of Europe, Convention on Cybercrime art. 4, *opened for signature* Nov. 23, 2001, E.T.S. No. 185.

[49] *Convention on Cybercrime*, COUNCIL OF EUROPE, http://conventions.coe.int/Treaty/Commun/ChercheSig.asp?NT=185 &CM=8&DF=28/10/2010&CL=ENG (last visited Mar. 1, 2012).

[50] *Id.*

[51] *Id.* art. 5.

[52] Elizabeth Montalbano, *Auditors Find DOD Hasn't Defined Cyber Warfare*, INFORMATIONWEEK (Sept. 14, 2010), http://www.informationweek.com/news/government/security/227400 359.

to intimidate any person in furtherance of such objectives."[53] The methodology of a cyber attack involves a deliberate action taken to "alter, disrupt, deceive, degrade, or destroy adversary computer systems or networks or the information and/or programs resident in or transiting these systems or networks."[54] Often, cyber attackers intend to destroy the entities reliant on a computer system or network rather than the computer system or network itself.[55]

By comparison, cyber exploitation is the use of a deliberate cyber action that seeks to extract confidential information from an adversary's computer system or network.[56] The goal of cyber exploitation is to obtain information from a computer network without the user's knowledge, which amounts to a modern form of espionage. Espionage is illegal under the domestic laws of most nations, but it is not illegal under international law.[57]

Throughout history, nation-states have undertaken espionage by using agents to infiltrate and collect information about adversaries. Now, states can obtain the same information without the risk and complexity associated with using agents. Just as cyber

---

[53] U.S. Army Training & Doctrine Command, DCSINT Handbook No. 1.02, Critical Infrastructure Threats and Terrorism, at VII-2 (2006).

[54] JOINT CHIEFS OF STAFF, DEPARTMENT OF DEFENSE DICTIONARY OF MILITARY AND ASSOCIATED TERMS, JOINT PUBLICATION 1-02, at 65 (2010, as amended through Jan. 15, 2002), http://www.dtic.mil/doctrine/new_pubs/jp1_02.pdf (defining "computer network attack," which is used interchangeably with "cyber attack").

[55] Comm. on Offensive Info. Warfare, Nat'l Research Council, Technology, Policy, Law, and Ethics Regarding U.S. Acquisition and Use of Cyberattack Capabilities 80 (William A. Owens et al. eds., 2009).

[56] *Id.* at 81.

[57] Roscini, *supra* note 8 at 93.

criminals use computer systems to enhance their illicit activity, so have state governments. (As one intelligence expert wrote, if you want to keep a secret, don't write it down.[58] The modern twist might be, if you want to keep a secret, don't make it digital.) Cyber espionage, defined as the "unauthorized probing of a target computer's configuration to evaluate its system defenses or the unauthorized viewing and copying of data files," is a low-cost and low-risk tool for state governments.[59] Using the same techniques that cyber criminals utilize for gaining confidential information—such as malware,

---

[58] Thomas Powers, The Man Who Kept the Secrets 165 (1983).
[59] Cyberpower and National Security 423–24 (Franklin D. Kramer et al. eds., 2009).

phishing,[60] and code injection[61]—state governments now engage in for intelligence and commercial espionage.[62]

Anecdotal evidence suggests that cyber espionage is a familiar practice among state governments. Electronic trespassers probe US defense networks thousands of times each day.[63] Israel is particularly direct about its exploration of cyber

---

[60] Typically, the cyber attacker sends spam E-mail that appears to come from a legitimate user or institution. The spam E-mail urges the recipient to click on a link, which leads the user to a fraudulent website designed to look legitimate or innocuous. When the user enters confidential information, the fraudulent website records the information the recipient enters and sends it back to the attacker. *See* KELLIE BRYAN ET AL., CYBER FRAUD: TACTICS, TECHNIQUES, AND PROCEDURES 27 (James Graham et al. eds., 2009).

[61] Code injection exploits a bug in computer program. An attacker injects code into a computer program to change its execution. Cyber criminals use vulnerabilities in commercial websites to introduce their own commands that will give them access to confidential information in the databases of websites. Most commonly cyber criminals target credit card information and social security numbers. Theoretically, a cyber attacker could employ a similar attack on "secure" databases that are connected to a government website. *See* James Verini, *The Great Cyberheist*, N.Y. TIMES, Nov. 10, 2010, http://www.nytimes.com/2010/11/14/magazine/14Hacker-t.html?_r=2&scp=1&sq=alberto%20gonzalez&st=cse.

[62] Corporations regularly report data breaches. These reports show that the cyber espionage direct efforts both at corporations with classified national security contracts and companies with proprietary information, seeking to obtain a competitive edge in the global economy—a security risk in its own right. In 2009, President Obama estimated that, "last year alone, cyber criminals stole intellectual property from businesses worldwide worth up to one trillion dollars." President Barack Obama, Remarks by the President on Securing Our Nation's Cyber Infrastructure (May 29, 2009), http://www.whitehouse.gov/the-press-office/remarks-president-securing-our-nations-cyber-infrastructure.

[63] William J. Lynn III, Deputy Secretary of Defense, Remarks at the Defense Information Technology Acquisition Summit (Nov. 12, 2009), http://www.defense.gov/speeches/speech.aspx?speechid=1399.

espionage tactics. The Israeli Defense Forces' chief of military intelligence Major General Amos Yadlin explained that "[u]sing computer networks for espionage is as important to warfare today as the advent of air support was to warfare in the 20th century."[64] Since at least 2002, China has directed cyber espionage toward the United States in what the Department of Defense has termed Operation Titan Rain.[65] One report states that China has already downloaded at least ten terabytes of data from the Non-classified Internet Protocol Router Network.[66] Ten terabytes is enough space to store the entire printed collection of the Library of Congress in digital format. Additionally, cyber exploitation can serve as a modern form of reconnaissance that lays the groundwork for other forms of attack.

Nevertheless, cyber espionage and exploitation fails to rise to the level of warfare because the purpose or outcome of both cyber espionage and exploitation is to monitor information and not to affect a computer system's functionality. The possibility of using cyber exploitation as a precursor to a cyber attack raises a separate set of legal questions beyond the scope and purpose of this Article. Although similar to traditional espionage in that cyber espionage may violate any number of domestic laws or international agreements, it does not violate international laws of war. Therefore, as used here, "cyber attacks" will not refer to espionage or reconnaissance performed via cyber exploitation.

---

[64] David Eshel, *Killer Apps*, Def. Tech. Int'l, Feb. 1. 2010, at 39, http://www.military.com/features/0,15240,210486,00.htm; *see also* David A. Fulghum et. al., *Cyber-Combat's First Shot*, Aviation Week & Space Tech., Nov. 25, 2007, at 28, http://www.aviationweek.com/aw/generic/story.jsp?channel=defense&id=news/aw112607p2.xml.

[65] Kramer, *supra* note 59, at 85.

[66] *Id.*

II. THE LAWS OF WAR IN CYBERSPACE

The laws of war provide the framework for when it is acceptable to resort to the use of force (*jus ad bellum*) and governs the limits of acceptable wartime conduct (*jus in bello*). Together, international treaties and customary international law articulate the principles that nations rely upon to determine the lawfulness of their forceful conduct. The first section has two parts and examines the framework of *jus ad bellum* to assess (1) whether cyber attacks violate the general prohibition on the "use of force" under Article 2(4) of the United Nations (UN) Charter, and (2) whether a cyber attack can reach the threshold of "armed attack" that triggers the right to self-defense under Article 51. The second section examines the consequences under international law of hostile cyber operations that do not rise to the level of an armed attack. The final section evaluates the *jus in bello* regime, which governs the conduct of warfare, to determine how cyber attacks should operate under the law of armed conflict.

A. JUS AD BELLUM—RECOURSE TO FORCE

1. DO CYBER ATTACKS VIOLATE THE GENERAL PROHIBITION ON THE USE OF FORCE?

Article 2(4) of the UN Charter declares that "[a]ll Members shall refrain in their international relations from the threat or *use of force* against the territorial integrity or political independence of any state, or in any other manner inconsistent with the Purposes of the United Nations."[67] Determining whether a cyber attack violates this general prohibition on the use of force requires an understanding of 1) how force is interpreted in international law, and 2) whether cyber

---

[67] U.N. Charter art. 2, para. 4 (emphasis added).

attacks can reach the appropriate level under those standards.[68]

One place to begin this analysis is the Vienna Convention on the Law of Treaties, which provides the rules of treaty interpretation. Although adopted after the Charter, international law experts generally agree that the Convention's rules reflect customary international law.[69]

Article 31 of the Convention states that "[a] treaty shall be interpreted in good faith in accordance with the ordinary meaning to be given to the terms of the treaty in their context and in the light of its object and purpose."[70] The ordinary meaning of "force" is broad and encompasses conventional notions of kinetic attacks as well as other coercive measures.[71] Other coercive measures include: financial instruments, i.e., granting or withholding economic indulgences from a target; diplomatic instruments, i.e., negotiation and advocacy

---

[68] Even if a cyber attack does not rise to the level of force prohibited under Article 2, a cyber attack may still be inconsistent with international law. Massive Distributed Denial of Service (DDoS) attacks that target the business, government and commercial sectors of an adversary for a political purpose certainly constitutes a prohibited intervention. *See infra* notes 83–85 and accompanying text. The International Court of Justice states that "[t]he principle of non-intervention involves the right of every sovereign State to conduct its affairs without outside interference . . . it is part and parcel of customary international law." *See also* Military and Paramilitary Activities in and Against Nicaragua (Nicar. v. U.S.), 1986 I.C.J. 14 (June 27) (observing that the UN Charter does not cover the whole area of the regulation of the use of force).

[69] Georg Ress, *Interpretation of the Charter, in* THE CHARTER OF THE UNITED NATIONS: A COMMENTARY 13, 18 (Bruno Simma et al. eds., 2002).

[70] Vienna Convention on the Law of Treaties art. 31, *opened for signature* May 23, 1969, 1155 U.N.T.S. 331, 340.

[71] *Black's Law Dictionary* defines "force" as "power, violence, or pressure directed against a person or thing." BLACK'S LAW DICTIONARY 717 (9th ed. 2009).

between state representatives; and ideological or propagandistic instruments, which deploy carefully selected signs and symbols to relevant sectors of society with the design of influencing the governing elite.[72] Under a broad reading of "force," each of these instruments—military, economic, diplomatic, and ideological—could be subject to regulation under the Charter.

However, in light of the "object and purpose" of the Charter, "force" should be read more narrowly. The express aim of the United Nations is to maintain international peace and security, as well as "to save succeeding generations from the scourge of war."[73] That suggests the notion of force in 1945 was limited to the military instrument. The drafting history of the Charter reinforces this conclusion. The *travaux preparatoires* shows that a proposal *was* submitted to extend the scope of Article 2(4) to other strategic instruments— specifically, to economic coercion.[74] The United Nations ultimately rejected this proposal.[75] By explicitly excluding economic coercion from the definition of force in the drafting of Article 2(4), and implicitly rejecting ideological and diplomatic instruments as well, the drafters signaled that the determination of whether a nation has used force in violation of Article 2(4) focuses only on military instruments.

However, concluding that the Charter embraces a relatively narrow meaning of "force" does not end the analysis. Because the International Court of Justice (ICJ) has stipulated that the Charter does not encompass the

---

[72] W. Michael Reisman & James E. Baker, Regulating Covert Action 28–42 (1992).

[73] U.N. Charter pmbl.

[74] *See* Doc. 2, G/7 (e)(4), 3 U.N.C.I.O. Docs. 251, 252–53 (May 6, 1945) (Brazilian amendment proposals).

[75] *See* Summary Report of Eleventh Meeting of Committee I/1, Doc. 784, I/1/27, 6 U.N.C.I.O. Docs. 331, 334, 559 (June 4, 1945).

whole area of the regulation of force, and that it is appropriate to turn to customary international law to determine the regulation of force as well, this Article also references international agreements and decisions of the international court to discern how force is regulated under customary international law[76]

Cyber weapons are versatile and can be either a supporting actor in the theater of conflict or the main event. They are not monolithic weapons whose use leads to straightforward answers about whether they violate the prohibition on force. Rather, the innumerable harmful effects caused by cyber attacks make their categorization both more complex and more necessary. The effects of a cyber attack can range from a simple inconvenience (such as a DDoS attack that disrupts web traffic temporarily), to physical destruction (such as changing the commands to an electrical power generator causing it to explode), and even to death (such as disrupting the emergency lines to first responders so that calls cannot be made to police or ambulance services). But treating all forms of cyber attack as a use of force would require an implausibly broad reading of Article 2(4) that includes non-physical damage. A more nuanced approach is needed.

Another challenge is that the intensity and temporal scope of a cyber attack can transform an event from a low-level aggressive act to a prohibited use of force. In *Armed Activities on the Territory of the Congo*, (Dem. Rep. Congo v. Uganda), 2005 I.C.J. 116, 165 (Dec. 19), the ICJ determined that a violation of Article 2(4) resulted from the "magnitude and duration" of

---

[76] Military and Paramilitary Activities in and Against Nicaragua (Nicar. v. US), 1986 I.C.J. 14 (June 27) (observing that the United Nations Charter, the convention to which most of the United States' argument is directed, does not cover the whole area of the regulation of the use of force in international relations because customary international law continues to exist alongside treaty law).

Uganda's actions.[77] Therefore, magnitude and duration of an attack are appropriate factors for consideration in any model that analyzes the coercive tactics employed by a state. Beyond these factors, several possible models exist for determining whether a cyber attack rises beyond mere coercion to a use of force.

The first approach to analyzing force is to examine the method of delivery. Under this model, cyber weapons are categorized by the specific method of delivering an attack on an adversary. Whether it is a virus, worm, network intrusion, or some other cyber attack, this model prohibits cyber attacks based on how they are executed. The severe damage that particular types of cyber attack can inflict worldwide relative to the limited effects of narrowly designed exploits provides the basis for this approach. Of course, certain cyber weapons are inherently more destructive and dangerous than others. Under conventional warfare, specific treaties have already emerged around atomic, biological, chemical, and nuclear weapons. A convention that specifically regulates cyber weapons would be the natural evolution of weapons treaties. The challenge a cyber weapon-specific approach faces is that technology changes quickly; any international agreement deeming a particular type of cyber attack unlawful might be outdated by the time it is ratified.

The second approach to analyzing force views cyber weapons under a strict liability model. Adherents to this model deem any use of cyber attacks against

---

[77] Armed Activities on the Territory of the Congo (Dem. Rep. Congo v. Uganda), 2005 I.C.J. 116, 165 (Dec. 19) ("The unlawful military intervention by Uganda was of such a *magnitude and duration* that the Court considers it to be a grave violation of the prohibition on the use of force expressed in Article, 2 paragraph 4, of the Charter.").

critical infrastructure to be a use of force.[78] Many nations have already audited their critical infrastructure to determine where they are vulnerable to the consequences of a cyber attack.[79] The next step would be to authorize self-defense against cyber attacks that target critical infrastructure. Proponents of strict liability argue that it is an appropriate model because of the instantaneous and destructive nature of cyber attacks. Once a cyber attacker has targeted critical infrastructure, an imminent threat exists that, at least arguably, creates a sufficient level of harm to justify anticipatory self-defense.

The weakness of this model is that the effects of cyber attacks may be indiscriminate and uncontrolled once unleashed. Cyber attacks do not always intentionally target the critical infrastructure that they eventually disrupt. And even if a cyber attack targets critical infrastructure, such as the banking and finance system, the strict liability approach introduces interpretive difficulties by collapsing the distinctions between armed violence, coercion, and interference. Even more troubling is that a strict liability model would authorize self-defense for the most benign offenses.

The third approach to analyzing force examines cyber attacks as instruments equivalent to traditional kinetic weapons by looking at the direct results of an attack. If the result would be considered a prohibited use of force when caused by a kinetic weapon, then a cyber

---

[78] Walter Gary Sharp Sr., CyberSpace and the Use of Force 129-31 (1999).

[79] The United States, for example, has outlined several types of infrastructure—the physical and cyber assets of public and private institutions in agriculture, food, water, public health, emergency services, government, defense industrial base, information and telecommunications, energy, transportation, banking and finance chemicals and hazardous materials, and postal and shipping—the destruction or incapacity of which would cripple the nation's defensive or economic security. Roscini, *supra* note 8, at 117.

weapon should be no different. Thus, a cyber attack is a use of force if the attacker seeks to cause direct physical destruction, injury, or death. This approach removes the need to examine the instrument of delivery, and it allows the international community to adapt the Charter to evolving technology while accounting for nuances in the intensity of a cyber attack.[80]

The flaw in this approach is that most cyber attacks do not directly cause physical damage or death. For example, a cyber attack that temporarily shuts down the communication lines for emergency police and ambulance services may not cause physical damage or deaths directly, but it could easily cause both indirectly. Drawing the line between direct and indirect effects of a cyber attack is extremely difficult.

Michael N. Schmitt posits a model that has gained traction among legal scholars. Schmitt advocates for a consequence-based approach.[81] This framework requires examining whether the reasonably foreseeable consequences of a cyber attack resemble the consequences of a conventional attack. Schmitt provides six criteria for evaluating the consequences of cyber attacks on the target state: severity, immediacy, directness, invasiveness, measurability, and presumptive legitimacy. If the cyber attack shares enough commonalities in the six factors, extension of the prohibition on force is justified. The benefit of this model is that it addresses how to evaluate cyber attacks

---

[80] Ian Brownlie, INTERNATIONAL LAW AND THE USE OF FORCE BY STATES 362 (1963). This method also allows for the characterization of chemical and biological weapons as a use of force under the Charter despite the cause of injury and death from those weapons not being a kinetic result of the instrument.

[81] Michael N. Schmitt, Computer Network Attack and the Use of Force in International Law: Thoughts on a Normative Framework, 37 COLUM. J. TRANSNAT'L. L. 885 (1999).

that are coercive but do not directly result in physical damage, injury, or death.

Consider two examples from the widely reported Russian cyber attack on Estonia. During World War II, the Soviet Union placed a bronze memorial statue in Tallinn, Estonia. Estonians today view the statue as a symbol of Soviet occupation and political repression, while ethnic Russians in Estonia see the statue as a tribute to fallen Soviet soldiers. In April 2007, the Estonian authorities decided to remove the controversial statue. The result of this decision was two nights of mass protests and riots in Estonia known as "Bronze Night." In the weeks following Bronze Night, Estonia's digital infrastructure experienced a massive cyber attack originating mostly in Russia. Russian "hacktivists" [82] used massive DDoS attacks to target Estonia's web servers and bring web traffic to a halt.[83] Specific targets included news and government websites.

Under Schmitt's criteria, the severity of this cyber attack falls short of the use of force. While the cyber attacks were immediate, the consequences were minimal. There was no physical damage or measurable suffering. The disruptions mostly caused a temporary inconvenience. The disruption of web traffic caused by the attack was indirectly related to the likely intended coercive effect, which was to reverse the Estonian government's decision to remove the statue. The attack was intrusive and presumptively illegitimate, but the net results did not sufficiently resemble the use of force.

---

[82] Hacktivists are also popularly called "patriotic hackers."

[83] *A Cyber Riot*, THE ECONOMIST, May 10, 2007, http://www.economist.com/node/9163598; *War in the Fifth Domain*, THE ECONOMIST, July 1, 2010, http://www.economist.com/node/16478792; Arthur Bright, *Estonia Accuses Russia of 'Cyberattack'*, CHRISTIAN SCI. MONITOR, May 17, 2007, http://www.csmonitor.com/2007/0517/p99s01-duts.html.

One commentator astutely described the cyber attacks as being "more like a cyber riot than a military attack." [84]

There was, however, a cyber attack during this episode that brought down phone lines to emergency services, which presents a more troublesome scenario that jeopardized human life and limb. The severity of that cyber attack has consequences equivalent to a use of force. What matters in that cyber attack is not that it potentially inflicted severe consequences, but that it was liable to produce such consequences.[85] It can be assumed that the result of the cyber attack was immediate and created a measurable level of suffering for those who were not able to access police or ambulances in an emergency. In that instance, the cyber attack should rise to the level of force under Schmitt's framework despite the indirectness of its consequences.

These Bronze Night examples demonstrate that a consequence-based model is flexible enough to distinguish between different levels of attacks within the same conflict. In one instance, the consequence-based approach finds that a cyber attack should be considered forceful enough to be unlawful under Article 2(4). In the other, the consequences are too minimal to rise to the level of force. This model accounts for the nuances of a cyber attack's intensity without ignoring the indirect effects of a cyber attack. By comparison,, under the text of the Charter alone, neither cyber attack amounts to a prohibited use of force.

---

[84] Shaun Waterman, *Who Cyber Smacked Estonia?*, UNITED PRESS INT'L, June 11, 2007, http://www.spacewar.com/reports/Who_Cyber_Smacked_Estonia_99 9.html.

[85] *See, e.g.,* U.N. Security Council, 3245th mtg., U.N. Doc. S/PV.3245 (June 27, 1993) (demonstrating the support for the label of "armed attack" urged by the United States for the failed attempt to assassinate former President George H.W. Bush in 1993).

The deficiency of Schmitt's approach is that extending its principles outside the regime of cyber weapons introduces measures of coercion not traditionally included in the prohibition on force, such as economic, diplomatic, or ideological coercion. An alternative approach might be to scrap the Schmitt model altogether when the targets are economic, diplomatic, and ideological instruments of the state, which is not without precedent given that the Charter does something similar. (In the Charter, the military instrument is presumptively forceful in Article 2(4), leaving out the economic, diplomatic, and ideological modes of coercion.)

Another criticism of the Schmitt model is that it offers little guidance as to the weight of each of the six factors. Such indeterminacy will lead to variance in the rules of engagement in cyberspace. One way to slightly modify the Schmitt model is to tier the factors. For example, presumptive legitimacy should be a first-tier factor. Once a state has determined that an attack is not a legitimate use of force, the next tier to consider would be the severity and invasiveness of the attack. Following this, the immediacy, directness, and measurability of an attack would help a state determine whether a cyber attack is a prohibited use of force.

Because cyber attacks are so versatile and variable in their methods and purposes, a unilateral approach to regulation leaves much to be desired. There is no perfect method for analyzing cyber attacks with current technology. Effects-based models require a post-hoc analysis that may take days, weeks, or longer to determine the extent of an attack, which is an unacceptable timeframe for responding to an equivalent kinetic attack. But a strict liability model raises the possibility of wrongly escalating force in response to a low-level cyber atcyber attacktack. Technologies to identify and assess cyber attacks in real-time may eventually make this a moot point. Until then, classifying a cyber attack by a degree of force is only one of many hurdles for decision makers.

2. DOES A CYBER ATTACK REACH THE THRESHOLD OF "ARMED ATTACK" THAT TRIGGERS THE RIGHT TO SELF-DEFENSE UNDER ARTICLE 51 OF THE UN CHARTER?

When there is a conflict between nations, the Charter demands that members "[s]ettle their international disputes by peaceful means in such a manner that international peace and security, and justice, are not endangered."[86] Thus, the authority for a state's use of force originates either from the UN Security Council or by the state's right to act in individual or collective self-defense. The lingering question is whether cyber attacks can reach the threshold of "armed attack" that triggers the right to self-defense under Article 51 of the Charter. Article 51 states:

> Nothing in the present Charter shall impair the inherent right of individual or collective self-defense *if an armed attack occurs* against a member of the United Nations, until the Security Council has taken the measures necessary to maintain international peace and security.[87]

Is there a difference between an "armed attack" under Article 51 and a "use of force" under article 2(4)?

Some scholars argue that *any* use of force by regular armed forces constitutes a *per se* armed attack.[88]

---

[86] U.N. Charter art. 2(3).

[87] U.N. Charter art. 51 (emphasis added).

[88] *See, e.g.,* E. Wilmhurst, *Principles of International Law on the Use of Force by States in Self-Defense* (Chatham House International Law Working Paper 2005), http://www.chathamhouse.org.uk/files/3278_ilpforce.doc.

Under this view, any offensive action by a military cyber unit is an armed attack because it emanates from the armed forces of a state. The United States, China, Iran, Israel, and other nations around the world have already established military cyber units.[89] Offensive actions by these cyber units would be considered a *per se* armed attack that triggers the right to exercise individual or collective self-defense. The danger is that a single errant soldier could embroil a nation in a protracted conflict if his or her action permits the target state to respond in self-defense.[90] But this danger also exists outside the realm of cyberspace, so this concern represents a difference in degree rather than kind.

Others reject the *per se* approach, arguing that the ICJ's "scale and effects" test is more appropriate to determine when Article 51 is triggered. This is consistent with the ICJ's position that there is a substantive distinction between the "use of force" and an "armed attack." In *Military and Paramilitary Activities in and Against Nicaragua* (Nicar. v. US), 1986 I.C.J. 14, 202 (June 27), the ICJ defined the difference as primarily one of "scale and effects."[91] Thus, not every use of force warrants the exercise of the right of unilateral self-defense. To know whether a cyber attack meets the threshold of "armed attack" requires knowing

---

[89] Roscini, *supra* note 8, at 97-98.

[90] Armed Activities on the Territory of the Congo (Dem. Rep. Congo v. Uganda), 2005 I.C.J. 116, 214 (Dec. 19) ("According to a well-established rule of a customary nature, as reflected in Article 3 of the Fourth Hague Convention respecting the Laws and Customs of War on Land of 1907 as well as in Article 91 of Protocol I additional to the Geneva Conventions of 1949, a party to an armed conflict shall be responsible for all acts by persons forming part of its armed forces.").

[91] Military and Paramilitary Activities in and Against Nicaragua (Nicar. v. U.S.), 1986 I.C.J. 14, 202 (June 27).

where the de minimis threshold lies. However, this is a vague and fact-specific rule.

Under such a regime, interpretive power shifts to institutional bodies such as the United Nations and the ICJ. Perhaps it is ideal to involve the international community in determining whether a nation can rightfully respond in self-defense. But the "scale and effects" test also leaves a targeted state less guidance to determine whether an armed response is lawful.

Regardless of the scale or effect of an attack—whether it is kinetic or cyber—the type of weapon used in an "armed" attack is immaterial. In an advisory opinion concerning nuclear weapons, the ICJ referred to Articles 2(4) and 51, stating that "[t]hese provisions do not refer to specific weapons. They apply to any use of force, regardless of the weapons employed."[92] The Security Council reaffirmed this sentiment when it authorized the United States to respond forcefully in self-defense to the 9/11 attacks, where the "weapons" were hijacked airplanes. Thus, under the "scale and effects" test, a cyber attack could lawfully trigger the right of self-defense under Article 51 if it inflicts substantial destruction upon important elements of the target state.

So where does the de minimis threshold lie? Customary practice suggests that under conventional notions of force, even small-scale bombings, artillery, naval or aerial attacks qualify as "armed attacks" activating Article 51, as long as they result in, or are capable of resulting in, destruction of property or loss of lives.[93] By contrast, the firing of a single missile into some unpopulated wilderness as a mere display of force

---

[92] Legality of the Threat or Use of Nuclear Weapons, Advisory Opinion, 1996 I.C.J. 226, 244 (July 8).

[93] Y. Dinstein, War Aggression and Self-Defense 193 (2001).

would likely not be sufficient to trigger Article 51, despite violating Article 2(4).

What would the firing of a missile into unpopulated wilderness equate to in cyberspace? A cyber attack that merely creates an inconvenience might be a prohibited use of force, but it would not rise to the level of an armed attack. In comparison, a cyber attack capable of substantially destroying property or causing the loss of lives should trigger the right to self-defense.

Modern weapons—such as cyber weapons— have created new complications for states attempting to comply with the self-defense exception of the Charter. For example, when the Charter was written, weapons of mass destruction had yet to be developed. First strikes were incapable of the widespread destruction enabled by modern weapons. Today, states faced with strict compliance to Article 51 run the risk of total annihilation. Thomas M. Franck—a notable international law scholar—criticized the irrationality of the Charter's requirements, writing that "[t]aken literally, Articles 2(4) and 51 together seem to require a state to await an actual nuclear strike against its territory before taking forceful countermeasures. If this is what the Charter requires, then, to paraphrase Mr. Bumble, the Charter is 'a ass.'"[94] As Franck suggests, it is unreasonable to expect a state to comply with the Charter to the point of its total destruction.

The prospect of total or significant destruction has led states to turn to customary international law for the determination of when it is appropriate to forestall an attack. Under customary international law, anticipatory self-defense is a legitimate preemptive strategy. The *Caroline* test formulates the customary understanding of

---

[94] Thomas M. Franck, Who Killed Article 2(4)? Or: Changing Norms Governing the Use of Force by States, 64 AM. J. INT'L. L. 809, 820 (1970).

anticipatory self-defense. It states that for an action of anticipatory self-defense, a state must show that the "necessity of self-defense was instant, overwhelming, leaving no choice of means, and no moment of deliberation."[95] Even where each condition is met, forceful actions of anticipatory self-defense cannot be "unreasonable or excessive; since the act, justified by the necessity of self-defense, must be limited by that necessity, and be kept clearly within it."[96]

Sophisticated cyber attacks are designed to overwhelm a target state's computer systems instantaneously. There are, of course, cyber attacks that a state might foresee and counteract. A state might discover evidence of a cyber attacker's attempted network intrusion, an audit of computer systems might reveal unauthorized backdoors or malware, or targeted states might uncover an online forum that serves as a gathering place for hacktivists to trade information and tools prior to a coordinated attack. In such cases, the target state is previously aware of a planned cyber attack and may invoke its right to respond in anticipatory self-defense if the *Caroline* test criteria are met. Where met, a state might lawfully disable the servers that host the online forum where cyber attackers are gathering, assuming the state has no other means by which to forestall the imminent attack.

3. ATTRIBUTING STATE RESPONSIBILITY

Before a state responds in self-defense, several considerations must be weighed. One issue is whether the cyber attack should be treated as a law enforcement matter or a national security matter. Relevant to this determination is whether the level of force used in the cyber attack rises to that of an armed attack, as discussed

---

[95] R.Y. Jennings, *The Caroline and McLeod Cases*, 32 AM. J. INT'L. L. 82 (1938).
[96] *Id.*

in Section II(a)(ii). Another consideration is whether the state whence the attack originated is complicit. If the act of self-defense is not in immediate response to an ongoing attack, the state must impute responsibility before launching its cross-border counter-attack. Establishing state responsibility in the area of cyber attacks requires understanding states' duties to one another, particularly regarding non-state actors operating within their jurisdiction.

In 2001, the International Law Commission issued the Draft Articles on State Responsibility, which articulates the international jurisprudence on state responsibility. Article 1 states that "[e]very internationally wrongful act of a State entails the international responsibility of that State."[97] This notion of state responsibility is supported by state practice as well as *opinio juris*. In the *Corfu Channel Case*, (U.K. v. Alb.), 1949 I.C.J. 4 (Apr. 9), the ICJ examined the threshold to attribute responsibility for actions within a state's borders.[98] The ICJ held that territorial sovereignty is not only an essential foundation of international relations, but also that under customary international law, every state also has an obligation "not to allow knowingly its territory to be used for acts contrary to the rights of other states."[99] This formulation, however, does not account for the subtleties in degree of state responsibility. Should a state be held internationally responsible for a single soldier or patriotic hacker that uses a cyber attack to destroy critical infrastructure of an adversary? These questions merit further exploration.

---

[97] 2001 Draft Articles on the Responsibility of States for Internationally Wrongful Acts, U.N. Doc. A/CN.4/L.602/Rev. 1 art. 1 (July 26, 2001) [hereinafter State Responsibility].

[98] Corfu Channel Case (U.K. v. Alb.), 1949 I.C.J. 4 (Apr. 9).

[99] *Id.* at 22.

i.   State Actors

There is little controversy that, if a state's agent attacks another state, then the hostile conduct is attributable to the state. Article 4 of the Draft Articles on State Responsibility declares that "[t]he conduct of any State organ shall be considered an act of that State under international law."[100] A state organ is understood to be all the individual or collective entities that make up the organization of the state and act on its behalf.[101]

This principle is a codification of customary international law. It reflects the assumption that a state is fully responsible for its agents—even when those agents act outside the scope of their duties. In *Armed Activities on the Territory of the Congo*, (Dem. Rep. Congo v. Uganda), 2005 I.C.J. 116, 214 (Dec. 19), the ICJ held that "[a]ccording to a well-established rule of a customary nature . . . a party to an armed conflict shall be responsible for all acts by persons forming part of its armed forces." [102] This rule also applies to a person or entity that is not an organ of the state but nevertheless exercises elements of governmental authority.[103] This extends to private or public entities that a state may charge with elements of authority normally associated with the government. For example, if the British government employs private defense companies and

---

[100] State Responsibility, *supra* note 97, at art. 4.

[101] *Id.* art. 2 commentary.

[102] Armed Activities on the Territory of the Congo (Dem. Rep. Congo v. Uganda), 2005 I.C.J. 116, 214 (Dec. 19) ("According to a well-established rule of a customary nature, as reflected in Article 3 of the Fourth Hague Convention respecting the Laws and Customs of War on Land of 1907 as well as in Article 91 of Protocol I additional to the Geneva Conventions of 1949, a party to an armed conflict shall be responsible for all acts by persons forming part of its armed forces.").

[103] State Responsibility, *supra* note 97, at art. 5, 8; *see* Hyatt Int'l Corp. v. Iran, 9 Iran-U.S. C.T.R. 72, 88-94 (1985).

authorizes them to conduct active defense measures, the conduct of the private defense company is imputed to Britain. As the Commentary to the Draft Articles on State Responsibility notes, "[i]f it is to be regarded as an act of the State for purposes of international responsibility, the conduct of an entity must accordingly concern governmental activity and not other private or commercial activity in which the entity may engage."[104] This formulation is consistent with the "effective control" test discussed earlier. Similarly, a state may not coerce another state to do its bidding without accountability. Article 17 of the Draft Articles on State Responsibility holds a state internationally responsible for wrongful acts that "it directs and controls another State in the commission of," if the state exercising the direction and control does so knowingly.[105] This test hearkens back to the era of the *Corfu Channel Case* and its mandate that a state not knowingly allow an attack to originate from its territory. This is particularly important in the area of cyber attacks because of their surreptitious and uncontrollable nature.

As mentioned, many states have already begun developing cyber units within their military or intelligence apparatuses. States have also delegated some elements of their cyber attack capabilities to the private sector. One state might even consider using *another* state to launch an attack on its behalf. Although tracing a cyber attack is a formidable technical challenge, if the target state successfully traces a cyber attack to the source state's cyber unit or to an entity acting with the authority or under the control of the source state, the latter ought to be held responsible.

---

[104] State Responsibility, *supra* note 97, at art. 5.
[105] *Id.* at art. 17.

ii.   Non-State Actors

A harder question, in both the realm of cyberspace and traditional warfare, is determining whether it is appropriate to attribute state responsibility when non-state actors perpetrate an attack. Article 51 of the Charter does not provide instruction on whether a state may respond with force to a non-state actor. Non-state actors, usually hacktivists, present a complicated issue for targeted states.

Hacktivists are usually private citizens motivated by nationalistic or ideological feelings who possess sufficient skill to participate in a cyber attack. The nature of cyberspace permits hacktivists to launch attacks on from anywhere, at will, without government direction. Hacktivists' freedom to engage in cyber attacks from virtually anywhere in the world allows them to operate from the territory of a third party. Any action taken against a hacktivist in the territory of a third party state raises questions about violating that state's sovereignty, as well as whether the third party state has certain rights and obligations. The Charter does not explicitly address this facet of international conflict, leaving a legal loophole that hacktivists might exploit.

Yet custom and practice demonstrate that states can—and do—respond with force to non-state actors. The international response to the 9/11 attacks on the United States validated this principle of customary international law. After 9/11, the Security Council passed Resolution 1368, which reaffirmed the "inherent right" of the United States to respond in self-defense in accordance with Article 51 of the UN Charter.[106] Weeks later, when it was clear that non-state actors had committed the 9/11 attacks, the United States still

---

[106] S.C. Res. 1368, U.N. Doc. S/Res/1368 (Sept. 12, 2001) (Threats to International Peace and Security Caused by Terrorist Acts).

received nearly universal support, including from the Security Council, when it invoked its right to respond in self-defense.[107]

On what basis do we attribute responsibility to a state for the actions of its non-state actors? If the state directs or controls the non-state actors, regardless of whether the non-state actors are within its jurisdiction, there are several bases for which to hold the state responsible. However, "lone wolf" hacktivists—those who act without endorsement of the state—are a different matter.

Under the original *Corfu Channel* formulation, if a state may not knowingly allow its territory to be used for acts that violate another state's rights, then *mutatis mutandis* a state may not knowingly allow non-state actors within its borders to attack another state. More recently, the Articles on State Responsibility augment the *Corfu Channel* test by imputing responsibility to a state if "the person or group of persons is in fact acting on the instructions of, or under the *direction or control* of, that State in carrying out the conduct."[108]

The Articles on State Responsibility articulates the rule of the *Nicaragua* case. In *Nicaragua*, the issue brought before the ICJ was whether the United States was responsible for the actions of the contra guerillas in their rebellion against the Nicaraguan government. The Court held that to find the United States responsible would require "effective control" over the non-state actor group and also the exercise of that control with respect to the specific operation in which breaches were committed.[109] Such a finding would imply that state

---

[107] S.C. Res. 1373, U.N. Doc. S/Res/1373 (Sept. 28, 2001) (Threats to International Peace and Security Caused by Terrorist Acts).

[108] State Responsibility, *supra* note 97, at art. 8 (emphasis added).

[109] *Nicar. v. U.S.*, 1986 I.C.J. at 202.

control extends beyond its immediate territory. Thus, if a state is in "effective control" of non-state actors operating in another territory, it may be held responsible for their actions. The Declaration on the Strengthening of International Security proclaims that every State has the duty to refrain from organizing, instigating, or participating in acts of civil strife or terrorist acts *in another state*. Under this standard, if a state organized, assisted, and controlled hacktivists as proxies, responsibility for their agents' actions is imputed to the state with respect to the specific operations "controlled" by the state, wherever they might occur.

On the other hand, the International Criminal Tribunal for the Former Yugoslavia articulated a lower "overall control" test in *Prosecutor v. Tadic,* Case No. IT-94-1-T, Sentencing Judgment, ¶ 120 (July 14, 2007).[110] The *Tadic* tribunal acknowledged that this standard "to some extent equates the group with State organs proper."[111] The *Tadic* standard was applied only to participants in an organized and hierarchically structured group, such as a military or paramilitary force.

An example of such a paramilitary group is the Russian Business Network, which is often associated with Russia's political and military elite, though it is not a formal participant. The Russian Business Network was intimately involved in the cyber attacks on Estonia and Georgia, attacks for which Russia denied its own

---

[110] Prosecutor v. Tadic, Case No. IT-94-1-T, Sentencing Judgment, ¶ 120 (July 14, 2007). This lower standard was criticized by the ICJ in the *Genocide Case* as being unsuitable because it "has the major drawback of broadening the scope of State responsibility well beyond the fundamental principle governing the law of international responsibility." Case Concerning the Application of the Convention on the Prevention and Punishment of the Crime of Genocide (Bosn. & Herz. v. Serb. & Montenegro), Judgment, 2007 I.C.J. 43 (Feb. 26).

[111] *Tadic*, Case No. IT-94-1-T, at ¶ 121.

involvement. Under the "overall control" test, the relationship between the Russian Business Network and the Russian State should be sufficient to impute state responsibility.

As for individuals and unorganized groups, the *Tadic* tribunal accepted the higher "effective control" standard to impute state responsibility. In order to meet the "effective control" test, the *Tadic* tribunal determined that there must be "specific instructions or directives aimed at the commission of specific acts," or, in the absence of direction, that there be a public endorsement of the acts *ex post facto*.[112] Article 11 of the Draft Articles on State Responsibility declares that "[c]onduct which is not attributable to a state under the preceding Articles shall nevertheless be considered an act of that State under international law if and to the extent that the State acknowledges and adopts the conduct in question as its own."[113]

The *United States Diplomatic and Consular Staff in Tehran (U.S. v. Iran)*, 1980 I.C.J. 3 (May 24), case is evidence of this principle in practice. The seizure of the US embassy and its personnel by militants was endorsed by the Iranian State. The ICJ held that Iran's approval translated into state responsibility for the actions of the militants. Under this framework, if individuals or unorganized groups of hacktivists use a cyber attack to destroy a power plant in another state and their host state unequivocally approves the action, the attack will be imputed to that host state.

The hardest question for state attribution is whether a state is responsible for lone wolf hacktivists that operate without active encouragement from a state. In this scenario, international law requires states to take reasonable preventive measures. The Convention on

---

[112] *Id.* at ¶ 132.
[113] State Responsibility, *supra* note 97, at art. 11.

Cybercrime, for instance, requires signatories to adopt domestic laws that criminalize cyber attacks. How far a state's duty extends to prevent lone wolf hacktivists remains undetermined. For instance, must a state adapt its technology in some way, for example by removing online anonymity? Such a requirement raises serious questions about the liberty and privacy interests of individuals. But this is an issue that is more clearly within the range of domestic law, rather than the laws of war, and thus outside the scope of this Article.

What if a state were required by international law to take reasonable measures to protect other states from foreseeable cyber attacks? Under that standard, a state that knows of cyber attackers launching attacks must take reasonable steps to fulfill its duty, by stopping the attacks, bringing the attackers to justice, or preventing further attacks. If a state does not cooperate, the targeted state may respond unilaterally in self-defense under Article 51. If a state knowingly allows— either through action or omission—a non-state actor to commit an attack, the state would be held internationally responsible. But if the state undertakes sufficient measures to protect other states, and a cyber attack still manages to originate from its territory, the state would not be responsible.

Since the 9/11 attacks, scholars argue that there has been a shift in the doctrine on state responsibility.[114] Arguably, pre-9/11, a state would be held responsible for the actions of hacktivists operating within its territory if it could be shown that the state exercised "effective control" over them. State responsibility did not extend to knowingly harboring perpetrators of attacks. Since 9/11,

---

[114] Sonja Cenic, State Responsibility and Self-Defence in International Law Post 9/11: Has the Scope of Article 51 of the United Nations Charter Been Widened as a Result of the US Response to 9/11?, 14 AUSTL. INT'L L.J. 201 (2007).

this understanding of state responsibility has been challenged. Evidence of this change is seen in the overwhelming international support for the US campaign against Al-Qaeda.[115] This change is perhaps best encapsulated by the Security Council's adoption of Resolutions 1368 and 1373.[116] In Resolution 1368, the Security Council explicitly stated that those who aided, supported, or *harbored* the perpetrators of the 9/11 attacks would be held accountable.[117]

This view of state responsibility remains controversial. It suggests a remarkable shift from the standards articulated in *Nicaragua* and *Tadic*. Those who dispute the shift in the doctrine of state responsibility claim that the Security Council resolutions were an exceptional response to an exceptional set of circumstances. Perhaps, however, the international response can also be explained on the grounds that harboring the perpetrators of the 9/11 attacks is similar to endorsing their actions, which implies that the state is knowingly in violation of its duty to prevent attacks from its territory.

This change puts a high burden on states in the realm of cyberspace without any direction as to compliance. Cyber attacks can be executed from virtually anywhere, meaning that every state could potentially be held internationally responsible, even where its only nexus to the attack was the attacker's presence on its soil for the moment that it took to plug in and execute the attack.

Regardless of which standard is used, a state may not attribute state responsibility and then

---

[115] *Id.* (discussing support for the American military campaign in Afghanistan).

[116] S.C. Res. 1368, *supra* note 106; S.C. Res. 1373, *supra* note 107.

[117] S.C. Res. 1368, *supra* note 106 (emphasis added).

immediately respond with force. Rather, the victim state must request that the offending state comply with its international obligations.[118] If the offending state does not comply, the targeted state may impute state responsibility and act accordingly.

B. CYBER ATTACKS NOT COVERED BY JUS AD BELLUM

Cyber attacks that rise to the level of a prohibited use of force or that cross into the threshold of armed attack are regulated by *jus ad bellum*, which was designed to govern warfare. This Section, however, will examine how to regulate cyber attacks that fall below the level of a use of force and are consequently not covered by *jus ad bellum* protections. It is divided into two parts: the first part discusses cyber attacks that involve the use of economic, diplomatic, or ideological instruments. The second part examines low-intensity cyber attacks involving the use of the military instrument.

1. COERCIVE NON-MILITARY INSTRUMENTS IN CYBERSPACE

Low-intensity conflicts are conducted using the four strategic modes discussed previously: military, economic, diplomatic, and ideological. Regardless of whether these instruments are used as a tool of persuasion or coercion, their intended outcome is to influence the behavior of the targeted state. While the Charter deals primarily with the military instrument,

---

[118] Gabcikovo-Nagymaros Project (Hung. v. Slovk.), 1997 I.C.J. 7, 55-56 (Sept. 25) ("In the first place [countermeasures] must be taken in response to a previous international wrongful act of another State and must be directed against that State. . . . Secondly, the injured State must have called upon the State committing the wrongful act to discontinue its wrongful conduct or to make reparation for it. . . . [Third] the effects of a countermeasure must be commensurate with the injury suffered, taking account of the rights in question.").

cyber attacks are versatile enough to fit within the other modes. This Section will examine the following scenarios using the non-military modes of coercion—economic, ideological, and diplomatic—and how international law might govern them:

Economic: A cyber attacker takes the New York Stock Exchange offline to undercut confidence in the integrity of the American financial markets.

Ideological: A cyber attacker manipulates the Internet pages of American politicians to associate them with radical positions with the intention of undermining their domestic political support.

Diplomatic: A cyber attacker steals classified cables from the US Department of State and publishes them online to embarrass the diplomatic corps of the United States.

i.   The Economic Instrument

Hackers already appear to have penetrated into the computer systems that control the New York Stock Exchange.[119] While no damage appears to have ensued, these breaches illustrate the extraordinary opportunity for economic devastation. A cyber attack undermining the international community's faith in the financial markets would cause a vast economic disruption with worldwide ramifications. How might international law treat such an attack?

As previously mentioned, Article 2(4) did not categorize economic coercion as a prohibited use of force. Nowhere in the Charter is economic coercion prohibited. The Charter does, however, mention that

---

[119] Devlin Barrett, *Hackers Penetrate NASDAQ's Computers*, WSJ, Feb. 5, 2011, http://online.wsj.com/article/SB10001424052748704709304576124502351634690.html.

economic sanctions are permitted when called for by the Security Council.[120]

In practice, economic coercion is an accepted tactic in international relations. States regularly use loans, credits, and foreign aid, among other means, to influence state action in designed ways. As will be discussed, economic coercion is also an lawfully accepted method of deprivation that states use as a countermeasure, also known as retorsions. While domestic laws may prohibit covert methods of economic coercion such as bribes or payments for intelligence, there is no comparable prohibition in international law. Some experts argue that economic modes of coercion are welcome when the alternative is to resort to military force.[121] Note that this does not mean that economic coercion is unregulated or ought to be lawful; extreme forms of economic coercion ought to be unlawful.

W. Michael Reisman and James Baker III offer one explanation for the unlawfulness of such an extreme method of economic coercion. "[W]e would surmise that where the particular unilateral economic strategy raises costs as a means of securing desired behavior, it would be viewed as lawful. Where it would seriously undermine a political, economic or, if practiced widely, disrupt the international economic system, it would, like other *undiscriminating* strategies that injure unrelated parties, probably be viewed as unlawful."[122] An action that would strike the heart of the American economy would certainly rise to an indiscriminate strategy that injures an unacceptable number of non-combatant parties.

---

[120] U.N. Charter art. 41.

[121] Seid-Hohenveldern, *The United Nations and Economic Coercion*, 18 BELGIAN REV. INT'L L. 9, 12 (1984).

[122] REISMAN & BAKER, *supra* note 72, at 30 (emphasis added).

ii.   The Ideological Instrument

In previous cyber conflicts, cyber attackers have defaced the websites of political leaders as a form of psychological operation. The process of mischaracterizing politicians is regularly witnessed during election cycles. Would a state violate its international obligations by employing a cyber attack that discredited an American politician, e.g., by associating him or her with radical positions to undermine his or her support, thereby intervening in the United States' political process?

The ideological instrument is an attempt by an external actor to influence the body politic of a state for the purpose of changing its behavior. The democratic nature of cyberspace makes it particularly vulnerable to the ideological instrument. Virtually anyone can access the Internet, allowing a message to gain widespread traction more easily than traditional measures of propaganda. The combination of the worldwide audience and the ease with which a cyber attacker can implant a message makes cyberspace a fertile ground for using the ideological instrument.

The ideological instrument presents a struggle between free speech and a state's responsibility to promote non-interference in the affairs of other states. While the Charter is silent on the use of the ideological instrument as a method of coercion, a number of international agreements restrict or limit the use of the ideological instrument for hostile purposes.

The General Assembly has set forth its view of propaganda. In Resolution 110, the international body "condemns all forms of propaganda . . . which is either designed or likely to provoke or encourage any threat to the peace, breach of the peace, or act of aggression."[123]

---

[123] G.A. Res. 110 (II), at 88-93, 1947-1948 U.N.Y.B. 14 (Nov. 3, 1947).

Subsequent resolutions have also sought to proscribe conduct for "war mongering" and "hostile propaganda."[124] State practice, however, demonstrates that these resolutions have little to no effect on state conduct. Thus, the international community has not come to a workable resolution of the tension between a state's promotion of domestic free speech and a state's responsibility to adhere to the principle of non-interference.

There are several well-known convictions for violations of the prohibition on inciting violence through propaganda. Notably, these convictions arise in the context of genocide. In the Nuremberg Trials, the newspaper publisher and author Julius Streicher was convicted for a crime against humanity for inciting murder and extermination in World War II.[125] In *Prosecutor v. Jean Paul-Akayesu*, Case No. ICTR 96-4-T (Sept. 2, 1998), the International Criminal Tribunal for Rwanda determined that Akayesu intended to incite genocide against the Tutsi group in Rwanda.[126]

Outside of genocide, the operational mode of international law as it relates to the ideological instrument is an *ad hoc* approach more concerned with the method of communication and how it is controlled than the effect of its content. Thus, a cyber attacker that sought to influence the internal body politic of an adversary by manipulating the webpages of American politicians to associate them with radical positions is likely a lawful action under international law. The same

---

[124] Declaration on the Inadmissibility of Intervention and Interference In the Internal Affairs of Sates, II(j); G.A. Res. 2625 (Declaration on Friendly Relations).

[125] The Trial of German Major War Criminals: Proceedings of the International Military Tribunal Sitting at Nuremberg Germany, Part 22, 501-2 (1950).

[126] Prosecutor v. Jean-Paul Akayesu, Case No. ICTR 96-4-T (Sept. 2, 1998).

action might nevertheless be unlawful under domestic criminal laws.

The action's lawfulness does not stop a state from responding with proportional countermeasures to a hostile cyber attack, which could create tension between a state's countermeasures and the promotion of free speech. The danger lies in the possibility that the internal elite will resort to a restriction on free communication when it is used to threaten their power. The potential threat to free speech should encourage a state to restrain itself in how broadly it interprets a cyber operation that involves the ideological instrument.

iii.   The Diplomatic Instrument

The diplomatic instrument consists of communication among the elites of nation-states and international organizations. Operationally, elites conduct much communication in secret, without domestic or international appraisal. Although the end product often results in a public international agreement, the process necessarily involves a high level of confidentiality.

Customary practice and treaties prohibit the use of coercion against diplomats. The protection extends in varying degrees to a diplomat's person, papers, personal property, facilities, communications, and movements. Article 29 of the Vienna Convention on Diplomatic Relations states: "The person of the diplomatic agent shall be inviolable. He shall not be liable to any form of arrest or detention. The receiving State shall treat him with due respect and shall take all appropriate steps to prevent any attack on his person, freedom or dignity." A similar protection applies to consular posts under the Vienna Convention on Consular Relations. Furthermore, the Convention on the Prevention and Punishment of Crimes against Internationally Protected Persons, Including Diplomatic Agents, extends protection from coercion to heads of state, foreign ministers, and any representatives of a state or international organization entitled to special protection under international law when a protected person is in a foreign state.

The nearly universal condemnation of violations against the diplomatic instrument of a state shows that a cyber attacker that steals classified cables from the US Department of State and then publishes them online to embarrass the US diplomatic corps would be in violation of international law. Such an attack would surely violate the dignity of the diplomat and his or her papers.

Each of the above is an example of a non-military action facilitated by a cyber attack. Technology permits a hostile state to act more quickly, inexpensively, and with a larger projection than in the past. Yet, the traditional governing regimes still apply. Moving coercive actions online does not mean that the actions are now unregulated; the traditional instruments that govern the economic, diplomatic, and ideological modes still apply. Hostile actions prohibited offline are equally prohibited if committed in cyberspace.

2. LOW-INTENSITY USES OF THE MILITARY INSTRUMENT IN CYBERSPACE

In many instances, despite a hostile or tense relationship, a cyber attack is not sufficiently grave for the *jus ad bellum* regime to govern. Low-intensity cyber attacks have consequences that are not significant enough to pass the de minimis threshold that triggers the right of a state to respond in self-defense under Article 51. While the action might be considered a prohibited use of force, the cyber attack may be insufficiently grave to warrant unilateral action. Even fewer guidelines exist insofar as a low-intensity cyber attack falls below the "use of force" threshold. But even these actions are subject to regulation through human rights law and international treaties.

Human rights law may impede states that seek to coerce others through low-intensity cyber attacks. Article 17 of the International Convention on Civil and Political Rights (ICCPR) states that "[n]o one shall be subjected to arbitrary or unlawful interference with his privacy, family, home or correspondence, nor to unlawful attacks on his honour and reputation."[127] Cyber attackers that gain remote-access to a user's computer files or that falsify electronic records to besmirch an individual run afoul of this ICCPR provision

Another problematic area of human rights law for cyber attackers is Article 19, which prohibits cyber that obstruct communication. Article 19 states that "[e]veryone shall have the right to freedom of expression; this right shall include freedom to seek, receive and impart information and ideas of all kinds, regardless of frontiers, either orally, in writing or in print, in the form of art, or through any other media of his choice." Cyber attacks that inhibit access to the Internet or other telecommunications—such as a DDoS attack—violate Article 19. Enforcement, however, presents a significant challenge to cyber attack victims, which is a characteristic problem of human rights law. Again, the difficulties of international actors in cyberspace are not so different from the troubles of conventional international law.

How might a state respond to cyber attacks that do not trigger the right of self-defense? Does a targeted state have to absorb all low-intensity hostile actions without flinching or does international law permit a response? If a response is lawful, are there restraints on how a state may respond to low-intensity cyber attacks?

---

[127] International Covenant on Civil and Political Rights, G.A. Res. 2200A, art. 17, U.N. GAOR, 21st Sess., U.N. Doc. A/RES/2200 (Dec. 16, 1966), 999 U.N.T.S. 171 (entered into force Mar. 23, 1976).

Even without a clear set of rules, states can and do unilaterally respond to low-intensity cyber attacks that fall short of an armed attack. Thus, this Section considers what rules ought to apply for responding to low-intensity attacks.

A state may always respond to actions that it perceives to be hostile, so the question of where a cyber attack falls on the armed attack scale is moot. Rather, the question is, how might a state *lawfully* respond? The answer depends on the magnitude and duration of the attack. Under international law standards, countermeasures must comply with the principles of necessity and proportionality. Accordingly, although a cyber attack may not merit self-defense, a state may nonetheless respond to it in kind.

Customary practice permits countermeasures in response to low-intensity attacks.[128] Countermeasures consist of either retorsions or reprisals and they are not limited to responding to wrongs inflicted by armed force. Countermeasures often respond to both economic and political wrongs.

Retorsions are unfriendly but lawful actions. States undertake them to remedy a hostile action—like a low-intensity cyber attack—committed by an adversary. In the world of cyber attacks, such a remedial action might involve shutting off the hostile state's access to internal servers until the targeted state feels secure that no more cyber attacks are forthcoming.

In contrast, reprisals are actions that would be otherwise unlawful, but are a justified response to an adversary's unlawful actions. Before engaging in reprisals, a state must comply with several criteria. First, the state must be taking action in response to a wrongful

---

[128] REISMAN & BAKER, *supra* note 72, at 90.

action directed against it.[129] Second, the targeted state must have called upon the aggressor to discontinue his or her wrongful conduct or make reparation for it.[130] Third, the effects of the countermeasure must be commensurate with the injury suffered.[131] In essence, the countermeasure must consider the intention and consequences of the precipitating wrongful act.

For instance, in 2009, the United States publicly announced its intention to conduct a cyber war exercise known as Cyber Storm—to test the defense of computer networks—in collaboration with other nations including Japan and South Korea. Shortly after the announcement, the North Korea media responded by characterizing the pending exercise as a cover for an invasion. During the Fourth of July holiday, a botnet began a DDoS attack against US and South Korean government websites and international companies. Richard Clarke claims in *Cyber War* that during this attack US websites were hit with as many as one million requests per second. The attack was substantial enough to bring down the Department of Treasury, Secret Service, Federal Trade Commission, and the Department of Transportation web servers for some time over the following week.[132]

In such a scenario, the United States could lawfully respond with proportionate countermeasures.

---

[129] Report of the International Law Commission on the Work of its Thirty-first Session: State Responsibility, [1980] 2 Y.B. Int'l L. Comm'n 117, (1980) (quoting R. Int'l Arb. Awards, vol. 2, at 1056-57).

[130] *Id.*

[131] Gabcikovo-Nagymaros Project (Hung. v. Slovk.), 1997 I.C.J. 7, 55-56 (Sept. 25).

[132] *U.S. Eyes N. Korea for 'Massive' Cyber Attacks,* MSNBC (July 9, 2009), http://www.msnbc.msn.com/id/31789294/ns/technology_and_science -security/; Stan Schroeder, *Has North Korea Started the First Cyber War?;* Mashable (July 8, 2009), http://mashable.com/2009/07/08/north-korea-cyber-war/.

Retorsions would include the United States shutting down access to its servers from North Korean servers. The nature of botnets, however, makes this an unlikely scenario. Botnets often hijack computers all over the world, and shutting down access to domestic servers from all international communication is an overly broad response. Thus, the United States might turn to other methods of retorsions to remedy the attack. For example, the United States might publicly condemn North Korea for its actions.

At the same time, the United States might also undertake reprisals in response to North Korea's cyber attack. Once the United States or South Korea determines that the DDoS attacks rise to the level of a prohibited use of force, and if demands to discontinue or provide reparation are ignored, the United States could respond in kind with its own DDoS attacks against North Korea. However, cyber reprisals have little effect in states like North Korea that are less technologically reliant than the United States.[133]

The ICJ has acknowledged the existence of countermeasures as a lawful right of a state, although the international community has sought to limit armed reprisals.[134] In *Nicaragua*, the court stipulated that a state might respond with proportionate countermeasures to a prohibited use of force that does not reach the gravity of an armed attack.[135] In *Case Concerning Oil Platforms*

---

[133] *Cf.* Michael Breen & Joshua A. Geltzer, *Asymmetric Strategies as Strategies of the Strong*, PARAMETERS, Spring 2011, at 41 (explaining why cyber attacks against the United States qualify as true asymmetric strategies).

[134] Declaration on the Inadmissibility of Intervention and Interference In the Internal Affairs of Sates, II(j); G.A. Res. 2625 (Declaration on Friendly Relations) ("States have a duty to refrain from acts of reprisal involving the use of force.").

[135] Military and Paramilitary Activities in and Against Nicaragua (Nicar. v. U.S.), 1986 I.C.J. 14, 249 (June 27).

(Iran v. U.S.), 2003 I.C.J. 161, ¶ 64 et seq., Judge Simma explained that proportionate countermeasures "consist[] of defensive measures designed to eliminate the specific threat . . . at the time of the specific incidents," thereby indicating that countermeasures are subject to the limitations of necessity and proportionality. Another consideration is whether "less grave" attacks may be accumulated for the purposes of assessing a self-defense claim. In these instances, consecutive attacks are linked in time, source, and cause. The incidents on their own are not sufficient to trigger Article 51, but the cumulative effect can transform the series of incidents into an armed attack, so that a targeted state may respond in self-defense. A response is therefore not strictly limited to the event that changed the tide, but may look retrospectively at the accumulation of activity. Thus, a large-scale response may be appropriate to a series of accumulated small-scale cyber attacks. For many, such a possibility is unsatisfying. It suggests that the United States might respond to a DDoS attack with missile strikes, if the DDoS attack can be linked to a pattern of low-level cyber attacks.

This result, however, is similar to how states respond to cross-border hit-and-run tactics of non-state actors. If each incident were considered in isolation, the target state would have little recourse. It might act in reprisal against the state if the target state could attribute responsibility. But reprisal would require a proportionate countermeasure to the incident, which might be insufficient to deter future attacks. If a state is able to accumulate the events and exercise its right of self-defense, it is permitted to respond on a larger scale in a planned and coordinated effort against its attackers. This doctrine, while controversial, has been invoked by several states.[136] The ICJ even implicitly acknowledged the accumulation doctrine in the *Oil Platforms* decision. It noted that "the question is whether that attack, either in itself *or in combination* with the rest of the 'series of attacks" cited by the United States can be categorized as an 'armed attack' on the United States justifying self-defence."[137] The court ultimately concluded that, "[e]ven taken cumulatively," the incidents did not amount to an armed attack. Article 15 of the Draft Articles on State Responsibility assigns responsibility "when the action or omission occurs which, taken with the other actions or omissions, is sufficient to constitute the wrongful act."[138]

The accumulation doctrine is noteworthy in the realm of cyberspace. There have been relatively few—if any—cyber attacks that when taken in isolation amount to an armed attack. There are many examples, however, of a series of cyber attacks that target a state. A series of cyber attacks, if accumulated, may result in the targeted state exercising its right to self-defense under Article 51. But the threshold remains high and should still depend partly on the gravity of the individual cyber attacks. For example, the Russian cyber attacks on Estonia mentioned earlier comprised a series of incidents that lasted for several weeks, causing disruption in both communication and services in the public and private sectors. If Estonia had been able to attribute the attacks to Russia, Estonia might have invoked the accumulation doctrine with respect to the relentless cyber attacks. Whether the international community would consider the

---

[136] Tom Ruys, The Intangible 'Armed Attack': Evolutions in Customary Practice Pertaining to the Right of States to Self-Defence and the Quest for a Definition of 'Armed Attack' Under Article 51 UN Charter 259 (2009) (unpublished Ph.D. dissertation, Catholic University of Leuven) (on file with author).

[137] Case Concerning Oil Platforms (Iran v. U.S.), 2003 I.C.J. 161, ¶ 64 et seq. [hereinafter Oil Platforms].

[138] State Responsibility, *supra* note 97, art. 15.

accumulated attacks sufficient to trigger the right to respond in self-defense would depend on the magnitude and duration of the "less grave" exhibitions of cyber attacks. That test involves a high threshold that will be difficult for most victims of cyber attacks to demonstrate.

In practice, most cyber attacks fall below the threshold of an armed attack. Many even fall below the threshold of a prohibited use of force. This does not mean that states must stand by defenseless. States can, and do, respond, to coercive tactics undertaken by hostile states with countermeasures. But the responding state must first call upon the aggressor to discontinue its wrongful conduct or make reparations. The target state may respond only if the hostile state fails to comply with its request.

A state's response to low-intensity cyber attacks is nevertheless constrained. Any countermeasure is governed by the principles of necessity and proportionality. Thus, the effects of the countermeasure must be commensurate with the injury suffered. A state may only go beyond a proportionate countermeasure if they are responding to a series of attacks. Thus, while each individual attack remains below the threshold of an armed attack, taken together the attacks constitute an armed attack. Again, this threshold remains high in international law.

3.   COVERT CYBER ATTACKS

Due to the sensitive nature of national security, states do not widely disseminate information regarding their cyber capabilities. Secrecy is a necessary quality for an effective cyber attack. Without secrecy, the intended target may effectively defend or prevent an attack. Thus, there is little public information on the current stockpile of cyber weapons or how they are used in practice.

What the public does know is that most cyber attacks occur covertly,[139] where the perpetrator is an unknown actor or where the cyber attack itself is unknown. The exposed "covert" operations—such as the cyber attacks on Estonia—are publicly known due to their widespread effects on civil society or because the attack had an observable physical manifestation. There is also the possibility that information regarding a cyber attack is deliberately unveiled to deter adversaries or because the victim publicly condemns the action.

Regardless of how the public learns of a cyber attack, the scraps of available public information indicate that a vast majority of cyber attacks is committed covertly, outside the context of war. Does an action's lawfulness change based on whether a perpetrator's identity is concealed? How should international law govern covert cyber operations?

There are times when secrecy benefits the international public order. For one, an outcome achieved without force by a covert operation avoids escalation into a military conflict and its attendant costs.

On the other hand, the danger of covertness lies in the lack of state accountability. For example, if a state overtly seeks to stop its adversary's nuclear weapon program, its adversary receives domestic and international public condemnation from others, who also wish to stop the nuclear weapon program. The element of transparency has two important functions for the regulation of force. First, the overt operation puts the adversary on notice of what actions it must take to cease

---

[139] "Covert" in this section refers to the target's inability to identify its attacker. While "covert" may also refer to a state operation of which its constituents are unaware, this section will refer to "covert" in the former sense. While a serious issue that deserves further scrutiny, a state that conceals its operations from its domestic audience is more closely attached to domestic law and policy concerns.

the coercive actions. Second, the architect of coercion is held accountable in an overt operation, and its actions are subject to domestic and international public and legal appraisal. Neither function is present during a covert operation.

The prohibition on the use of force under Article 2(4) does not distinguish between covert and overt attacks. If one subscribes to the textual myth of the Charter, the element of covertness does not tip the scales of justice. The Charter does not articulate tiers of unlawfulness that account for the injustice to states unable to identify what actions must take place to cease a covert attack or hold their covert attacker accountable. Under the Charter, a prohibited armed attack is unlawful whether committed covertly or overtly, and the element of covertness generally does not factor into the determination of lawfulness.

Nonetheless, the element of covertness may transform an otherwise lawful operation into an unlawful attack. There are two areas that shed light on the lawfulness of covert operations. These are the prohibition on perfidious conduct and legitimate *ruses de guerre*.

The laws of war permit a state to engage in a *ruse de guerre*. *Ruses de guerre* mislead the adversary into making a tactical mistake by catching the adversary off-guard. As articulated in Article 37 of the first Additional Protocol, a state may engage in the use of camouflage, decoys, mock operations, and misinformation, among other tactics.[140] Secrecy and deception inhere to the effectiveness of these tactics. A cyber attack that employs a disinformation campaign by failing to secure misleading documents in military databases, such that an adversary steals false information, is a legitimate *ruse de guerre*. One of the

---

[140] Protocol I, *supra* note 46, art. 37.

incentives to employ a cyber attack is that its covertness gives an attacker a tactical advantage. After all, an enemy possesses no right to be notified before an attack, nor does the enemy possess the right to be free from surprise attacks or ambushes.

The deceptive tactics of the attacker, however, are still constrained. Article 37 of the first Additional Protocol prohibits killing, injuring, or capturing an adversary by resort to perfidy. The provision defines perfidy as "[a]cts inviting the confidence of an adversary to lead him to believe that he is entitled to, or is obliged to accord, protection under the rules of international law applicable in armed conflict, with intent to betray that confidence."[141] Among the enumerated examples of perfidy is the feigning of civilian, non-combatant status. Similarly, under Article 4 of the Third Geneva Convention, a state's forces must "carry arms openly" and have a "fixed distinctive symbol recognizable at a distance."[142]

In *Ex parte Quirin*, a group of German soldiers during World War II removed their uniforms so that they could slip into the United States in civilian clothing. The US Supreme Court held that while the intended targets— US war facilities—were legitimate and lawful targets, it was "the absence of uniform that render[ed] [the German soldiers] liable to trial for violation of the laws of war."[143] Thus, the nominal element of covertness *can* transform an otherwise lawful operation into an unlawful

---

[141] *Id.*

[142] Convention [No. III] Relative to the Treatment of Prisoners of War, Aug. 12, 1949, Art. 4, 6 U.S.T 3316, 75 U.N.T.S. 287.

[143] *Ex parte* Quirin, 317 U.S. 1, 15 n. 12 (1942).

action under international law.[144] The laws of war
tolerate ruses to mislead an adversary, but not to the
extent of misleading an adversary of one's status as a
non-combatant.

The purpose of these provisions is to make the
lawful combatants in a conflict identifiable so that a
targeted state may discriminate between lawful
combatants and civilians. The Commentary clarifies who
are combatants and who are civilians.[145] By separating
combatants and civilians into separate categories,
civilians are better protected and the evils of war are
mitigated.

To comply with the laws of war, a state must
ensure that its forces are distinguishable from the
civilian population. Those laws require combatants to
self-identify by means of a fixed distinctive symbol,
although they do not specify what else a state's forces
must do to comply. Although a fixed distinctive symbol
is often a uniform, it is possible that other symbols could
comply.

In cyberspace, however, the requirement to wear
a uniform does not make sense. But an identifying line
of code is both possible and consistent with the intent of
Article 4. However, both obligations within the Third
Geneva Convention apply to the cyber attacker and not
to the cyber weapon. A state could formally comply with
the strict language of this provision by having its cyber
attackers in uniform while safely tucked away thousands

---

[144] State practice does not always follow this standard. In World
War II, a British officer was commended for using civilian clothing
to infiltrate a German base to kill a general. W. Hay Parks,
Memorandum of Law: Executive Order 12333 and Assassination,
ARMY LAW, Dec. 1989, at 6.

[145] Jean de Preux, et al, The Geneva Conventions of 12 August
1949: Commentary: III Geneva Convention Relative to the Treatment
of Prisoners of War 46–47 (ICRC 1960) (Jean S. Pictet, ed.) (A.P. de
Heney, trans).

of miles away from the "battlefield," thereby reducing the distinctive symbol obligation to an empty requirement.

In practice, the operational norm is not aligned with the aspirational message of the Charter. Scholars such as W. Michael Reisman and James Baker III make the case that operations, which may be lawful if done overtly, might be unlawful if undertaken covertly.[146] Thus, some covert cyber attacks would be less permissible than identical overt cyber attacks.

Factors condition the international response to covert actions. Among these are whether the covert action (1) is executed through the military instrument or another mode of coercion; (2) involves independent and disproportionate violations of other norms governing violence; (3) is governmental or non-governmental; and (4) is a single operation or integrated into an overall mission.[147] Together, these factors influence whether the international community considers the covert nature of the action unlawful.

The laws of war are designed to regulate the use of force and moderate its consequences. Clear rules of how to operate on a battlefield—or in cyberspace— brings order to war and protection for noncombatants. To the extent possible, trust must exist that each participant is fighting under the same operational code. The absence of trust leads to escalating paranoia that encourages higher levels of violence and treachery, putting noncombatants at a greater risk.

Do covert cyber attacks put civilians at risk of being misidentified as the perpetrators? States have been wrongly accused of perpetrating a cyber attack, so it is conceivable that a reprisal or an act in self-defense

---

[146] REISMAN & BAKER, *supra* note 72, at 30.
[147] *Id.* at 67-72.

aimed at an accused state could cause civilian deaths.[148] Further, the scenario of a targeted state misattributing an attack to civilians and taking action in violation of international law is more likely in peacetime than in conflict. During a conflict, a cyber weapon operates like any other. Though it may cross into the threshold of perfidy, the element of covertness during a conflict should not transform an otherwise lawful attack into a violation of the laws of war. In a conflict, the participants are known. If a cyber attack occurs, it is likely attributed to the adversary state rather than to a civilian group, thereby mitigating the effects on civilian life of a countermeasure. A covert cyber attack that is executed during a conflict is less likely to raise questions than one where the targeted state is not on notice of what actions it may take to cease the operation.

The situation is different during peacetime. A state is not on notice of who is attacking or what actions it can take to stop an attack. Take, for instance, an action meant to coerce a country by targeting its economy. Economic coercion is necessarily overt. Such a strategy is meant to coerce rather than destroy. By acting overtly, an actor communicates a message designed to change the behavior of the target. A covert use of the same strategy delivers no message, as the targeted state will not know the identity of the actor. Without the identity, the targeted state is bereft of strategies it might adopt to terminate the action—does the state comply with the aggressor's demands or take countermeasures?

---

[148] In the 1998 Solar Sunrise attacks, computers based in the United Arab Emirates breached military computers in the United States. It was later reported that it was not an attacker actually from the United Arab Emirates behind the attack, but an Israeli teenager and two high school students from California. Christopher C. Joyner & Catherine Lotrionte, *Information Warfare as International Coercion: Elements of a Legal Framework*, 12 EUR. J. INT'L L. 825, 839 (2001).

Otherwise lawful conduct *executed covertly* ought to be factored into the lawfulness of a cyber attack during peacetime. Although, even if the element of covertness was given more weight during peacetime, a cyber attacker could post its demands anonymously, thereby reducing the effect of covertness in determining the lawfulness of the action.

The rules of engagement in cyberspace are still emerging. During this incipient stage, adversaries continue to test the tolerance of one another and the international community. Toleration for covert actions below a certain threshold has emerged as part of the current paradigm. States endure cyber attacks without resorting to international fora when the consequences are minimal and have little effect on the balance of powers.

Legal considerations of covertness will gain greater resonance as states increasingly employ covert cyber attacks to achieve their goals. There is no bright-line rule on whether a covert cyber attack will be held unlawful by the international community for the reason of its covertness. Whether a covert cyber attack is held unlawful depends on a number of contextual factors, including: (1) who perpetrates the attack, (2) who is the target, (3) whether civilians are at risk, (4) whether the intended outcome is to coerce or to destroy, (5) whether the target is afforded an opportunity preceding the covert operation to change its offensive behavior, (5) whether the attack complies with *jus in bello* obligations, and ultimately, (6) whether the covert cyber attack complies with the fundamental policies of the Charter.

C.   JUS IN BELLO: CONDUCT OF CYBER WARFARE

Once a state has entered into a conflict, the use of force is governed by *jus in bello*. Under *jus in bello*, even states that have the lawful right to use force still have limitations in how they use it. *Jus in bello* is largely derived from the Hague Conventions,[149] the Geneva Conventions,[150] and the associated protocols,[151] much of which is considered customary international law. In the words of the Saint Petersburg Declaration of 1868, the aim of the laws of war is to "alleviate as much as possible the calamities of war."[152] This section examines how the law of armed conflict ought to apply to cyber attacks. The restraints on how a state conducts its use of force is not contingent on the weaponry used, so transposing the principles of international humanitarian law to the use of cyber attacks—despite being a new weapon of warfare—is not only possible but also appropriate given its growing popularity as a coercive tactic. The following Sections will discuss the traditional schema of *jus in bello*—military necessity, distinction,

---

[149] Hague Convention IV Respecting the Laws and Customs of War on Land, Annex, Oct. 18, 1907, 36 Stat. 2277, 205 Consol. T.S. 277 [hereinafter Hague IV].

[150] *See* The Geneva Convention for the Amelioration of the Condition of the Wounded and Sick in Armed Forces in the Field, Aug. 12, 1949, 6.3 U.S.T. 3114, 3116, T.I.A.S. No.3362, at 3, 75 U.N.T.S. 31, 32 [GC I]; Geneva Convention for the Amelioration of the Condition of the Wounded, Sick and Shipwrecked Members of the Armed Forces at Sea, Aug. 12, 1949, 6.3 U.S.T. 3217, 3220, 75 U.N.T.S. 85, 86 [GCII]; Geneva Convention Relative to the Treatment to Prisoners of War, Aug. 12, 1949, 6.3 U.S.T. 3316, 3318, 75 U.N.T.S. 135, 136 [GC III]; Geneva Convention Relative to the Protection of Civilian Persons in Time of War, Aug. 12, 1949, 6.3 U.S.T. 3516, 3518, 75 U.N.T.S..287, 288 [GC IV] [all four hereinafter Geneva Conventions].

[151] *See* Protocol I, *supra* note 46; Protocol Additional to the Geneva Conventions of 12 August 1949, and Relating to the Protection of Victims of Non-International Armed Conflicts, opened for signature Dec. 12, 1977, U.N. Doc. A/32/144, *reprinted in* 16 I.L.M. 1442 (1977) [hereinafter Protocol II].

[152] Saint Petersburg Declaration Renouncing the Use, in Time of War, of Explosive Projectiles Under 400 Grammes Weight Preamble (1868), http://www.icrc.org/ihl.nsf/FULL/130?OpenDocument (last visited March 15, 2011).

proportionality, perfidy, and neutrality—in relation to cyber attacks.

1. MILITARY NECESSITY

When a cyber attacker is party to a conflict, international humanitarian law restricts the use of force to targets that will accomplish valid military objectives. Considered customary international law,[153] Article 52 of the Additional Protocol to the Geneva Conventions limits lawful targets to "those objects which by their nature, location, purpose or use make an effective contribution to military action and whose total or partial destruction, capture, or neutralization, in the circumstances ruling at the time, offers a definite military advantage."[154] Notably, Article 23 of the Fourth Hague Convention forbids destruction or seizure of property "unless such destruction or seizure be imperatively demanded by the necessities of war." Violating the principle of military necessity is considered a "war crime" in the Rome Statute of the

---

[153] *See, e.g.,* U.S. DEP'T OF ARMY, FIELD MANUAL 27-10: THE LAW OF LAND WARFARE 14 (2005); see also Michael J. Matheson, The United States Position on the Relation of Customary International Law to the 1977 Protocols Additional to the 1949 Geneva Conventions, 2 AM. U. J. INT'L L. & POL'Y 419, 420 (1987).

[154] Protocol I, *supra* note 46, art. 52; *see also* Case No. 47, *The Hostages Trial*, The United States of America vs. Wilhelm List, et al., United States Military Tribunal, Nuremberg, pg. 66, (ix) *The Plea of Military Necessity*, http://www.ess.uwe.ac.uk/wcc/List4.htm ("Military necessity permits a belligerent, subject to the laws of war to apply any amount and kind of force to compel the complete submission of the enemy with the least possible expenditure of time, life and money."); Oil Platforms (Iran v. U.S.), 2003 I.C.J. 161, ¶ 73 (Nov. 6) ("The requirement of international law that measures taken avowedly in self-defense must have been necessary for that purpose is strict and objective, leaving no room for any "measure of discretion").

International Criminal Court.[155] Valid targets are thereby limited to those objects contributing to an adversary's war efforts or those whose damage or destruction creates a definite military advantage.

A cyber attack that targets an adversary's military computer systems satisfies the condition of military necessity by virtue of their exclusive military association. There great opportunity to attack the computer systems of a modern military. Modern militaries use computer systems for every facet of operations.

But determining whether a target creates a "definite military advantage" is complicated. Presumably, this requirement limits cyber attacks with indeterminate military advantages. The complexity of computer systems makes calculating military advantage a challenge. The value of a cyber weapon often lies in its cascade effect on systems that rely upon the initial target. Most cyber attackers do not have sufficient information to predict the indirect effects of an attack. A cyber attacker that penetrates into the computer systems of an electrical generator *might* gain a military advantage, but the system may have unforeseen layers that prevent such an advantage from occurring. In these circumstances, the military advantage is not definite enough to satisfy the condition of military necessity.

Similar to conventional warfare, the conundrum is that cyber attacks could be deemed as creating a "definite military advantage" *ex post* whereas an *ex ante* analysis of the same attack might not come to the same conclusion. The definitiveness of the military advantage *ex post* is apparent only if the attack is successful. A cyber attacker could defend challenges to its use of force

---

[155] Rome Statute of the International Criminal Court, art. 8(2)(a)(iv), (1998), http://untreaty.un.org/cod/icc/statute/romefra.htm (last visited March 26, 2011).

by creating an information log that records what information the attacker knew about the target system at the time of attack. While the laws of war do not require such recordkeeping, an information log would be a relatively simple way to shield the attacker's decision to invoke military necessity to target an object.

Ultimately, the evaluation of whether a cyber attack arose from military necessity, will rely on a case-by-case determination. (This is similar to the evaluation of military necessity in traditional attacks.) In each instance, a cyber attacker must affirmatively determine that the attack offers a military advantage.

2. DISTINCTION

Military necessity is weighed against other limiting principles, including the principle of distinction. Article 48 of the Additional Protocol—considered a customary definition of distinction—requires attackers to "at all times distinguish between the civilian population and combatants, and between civilian objects and military objectives." Article 51 of the Additional Protocol requires attackers to ensure that "the civilian population and individual civilians . . . enjoy general protection against dangers arising from military operations" and "not be the object of attack."[156] Article 51, therefore, prohibits "indiscriminate attacks." Notably, the Rome Statute identifies the failure to distinguish between civilians and combatants as a "war crime." The purpose of distinction is to restrict attacks to combatants and military objectives only.

---

[156] Protocol I, *supra* note 46, art. 51; *see also* Protocol II, *supra* note 151, art. 13 (providing that "[t]he civilian population and individual civilians shall enjoy general protection against the dangers arising from military operations" and also "the civilian population . . . as well as individual citizens, shall not be the object of attack").

Civilians who directly participate in hostilities are not protected.[157] By virtue of participating, the civilian forfeits his protected status. But non-participating civilians sometimes die in attacks, and such civilian deaths are not *per se* war crimes. The principle of distinction allows for some civilian death as long as state makes reasonable efforts to distinguish between combatants and civilians, and to refrain from intentional attacks on civilians and civilian targets. The difficulty with making this distinction with respect to cyber attacks is that in cyber space, there is often an undefined and fuzzy line between military and civilian targets. (See, for example, the description in Section I(A) of how ARPA used the civilian infrastructure provided by AT&T to accomplish its goals.) To determine whether cyber attacks meet the requirements of distinction, a cyber attacker must establish (i) whether the attack sufficiently distinguishes between civilian and military targets, taking into account the dual-use of most Internet infrastructure, and (ii) whether the cyber attacks are conducted indiscriminately and without regard to the civilian population.

i.   Do Cyber Attacks Distinguish Between Civilian and Military Targets?

The laws of war are in place to ensure that parties to a conflict target combatants rather than civilians, and, if civilians are targeted, to ensure that such individuals have forfeited their protected status. To determine whether cyber attacks properly distinguish between civilian and military targets, one must understand where the distinction between the two lies.

Combatants consist of all *organized* armed forces, groups, and units that are under the command of

---

[157] Protocol I, *supra* note 46, art. 51.

the state.[158] These individuals may rightfully participate in hostilities. Under the law of armed conflict, combatants are required to distinguish themselves from the civilian population while they are engaged in an attack or in a military operation preparatory to an attack.[159] Non-combatants are understood to be civilians and enemy personnel out of combat.[160]

The definition of a lawful combatant under international humanitarian law requires a level of *organization* or state *command responsibility*. These traits are present within states with armed forces that have cyber capabilities. This also includes the *ad hoc* groups, such as the Russian Business Network, that receive implicit consent to act and, arguably, even direction from the state in their cyber attacks. The international humanitarian law definition of combatant is an awkward fit for cyberspace, where unorganized individuals can readily participate in cyber attacks against an adversary, as when hacktivists perform DDoS attacks for patriotic or ideological reasons. In those instances, should the targeted state be permitted to respond with a proportionate level of force? This is a pertinent question as cyber weapons become increasingly available to the masses.

In the realm of cyber war, hacktivists do not fall within the definition of lawful combatants and therefore are not treated as protected civilians under Protocol I "for such time as they take a direct part in hostilities."[161] Therefore, during the time that hacktivists participate in a conflict, they are valid targets. However, any use of force against them is limited by the principle of

---

[158] *Id.* art. 43.

[159] *Id.* art. 44(3).

[160] *Id.* art. 50(1).

[161] *Id.* arts. 47, 51 (3); *see also* Protocol II, *supra* note 151, art. 13.

proportionality. To the extent that hacktivists "carry arms openly" and are responding defensively, they could fit into the category of *levee en masse*, and receive Prisoner of War status under Article 4(a)(6) of the Third Geneva Convention, which extends protections to:

> Inhabitants of a non-occupied territory, who on the approach of the enemy spontaneously take up arms to resist the invading forces, without having had time to form themselves into regular armed units, provided they carry arms openly and respect the laws and customs of war.

What it means to "carry arms openly" in cyberspace is undefined as of yet. The efficacies of most cyber weapons stems from their ability to allow cyber attackers to penetrate a computer system undetected and inject their attack.

Cyber attacks often come quickly and without warning. There can be a significant lag time before the targeted state determines the source of the cyber attack. Regardless of a state's inclination to respond with force once it discovers the hacktivist source, it is prohibited from doing so if the hacktivist is no longer participating directly in the conflict. The relative ease with which civilians can participate in cyber attacks and remain undetected makes this limitation a true threat to targeted states. Such hacktivists momentarily become acceptable military targets, but they quickly return to their civilian status while remaining a potential threat. This problem can be partially addressed by shifting responsibility to states to prohibit, prevent, or stop cyber attacks from originating on their Internet infrastructure. States that do not comply would be internationally responsible. However, the level of control necessary for a state to comply with such a duty bumps up against the freedoms valued online. The proper balance of liberty in cyberspace and national security will be at the heart of future debate over regulation of cyber attacks.[162]

A related concern under the principle of distinction is when a cyber attacker forces a civilian to participate in a conflict. Civilian computers cannot ordinarily be classified as military objects unless they are participating directly in military activities. Cyber attackers can hijack civilian computers to incorporate them in a botnet attack against an adversary, thus involving these computers in military activities.

Such hijacking involves two violations. First, the cyber attacker unlawfully attacks civilian computers with malware that forces the computer to respond to the cyber attacker's command. The targeted state can then respond with a proportionate counter-attack against these hijacked computers, causing collateral damage to civilian infrastructure. In this case, the original cyber attacker is responsible for the subsequent damage to the civilian property caused by the targeted state. Second, the cyber attacker unlawfully forces civilians to participate in hostilities. Under the Fourth Geneva Convention, protected persons may be compelled to do

---

[162] *See, e.g.,* Jim Garamone, *Lynn Seeks Australian Cooperation in Cybersecurity,* AM. FORCES PRESS SERV. (Feb. 13, 2010) http://www.defense.gov/news/newsarticle.aspx?id=57951 ("We have the same tension you do between how do we balance between protecting this incredibly important national asset and protecting peoples' civil liberties and the right not to face governmental intrusion . . . We're still working through ways to balance that"); *see also Cybersecurity Discussion with General Keith B. Alexander,* CTR. FOR STRATEGIC & INT'L STUDIES (June 3, 2010), http://csis.org/event/cybersecurity-discussion-general-keith-b-alexander-director-national-security-agency ("We want to protect - some say the Constitution is not a suicide pact, and I agree, but it's also not something that we're just going to throw out our civil liberties and privacy. We were built on that. That's how our country was built. We want to ensure that we do our part to it. My responsibility, as the director of NSA, is to ensure that what we do comports with law.").

only work "which is not directly related to the conduct of military operations." [163] By creating a cyber weapon composed of civilian computers, a cyber attacker unlawfully forces civilians to participate in direct military operations. This is the cyber equivalent of a "human shield." DDoS attacks and social engineering tactics that involve civilians are questionable tactics that deserve exacting scrutiny to determine whether they violate international law principles.

Further, as previously suggested, distinguishing between civilian and military objects is complicated in cyber war.[164] Targeting purely military objects will not violate the principle of distinction. However, there are cyber attacks that deliberately target objects to kill civilians or destroy civilian objects. Such attacks are clearly unlawful under the law of armed conflict. In practice, however, cyber attacks targeting civilians have been more of an inconvenience than a threat to life or safety. For instance, in 2008, tensions arose between Georgia and Russia over the separatist regions of Abkhazia and South Ossetia. The conflict escalated into war in August of 2008. Along with kinetic attacks, cyber attackers operated from Russia. Massive DDoS attacks targeted Georgia's political websites using psychological warfare tactics, such as placing images of Adolf Hitler alongside pictures of the Georgian President. Hacktivists targeted media outlets and government websites during times of physical attacks, making communication particularly difficult and chaotic. Cyber attackers

---

[163] Geneva Convention Relative to the Protection of Civilian Persons in Time of War, Aug. 12, 1949, art. 40, 6 U.S.T. 3516, 75 U.N.T.S. 287; *see also* Geneva Convention Relative to the Protection of Civilian Persons in Time of War, Aug. 12, 1949, art. 147, 6 U.S.T. 3516, 75 U.N.T.S. 287. (explaining that a grave breach includes, "compelling a protected person to serve in the forces of a hostile Power").

[164] Protocol I, *supra* note 46, art. 52.

targeted CNN and BBC web servers in Georgia, blocking access to international news as well.[165] The attack on the media caused confusion. For the majority, however, the cyber attacks were only a temporary inconvenience. If the attacks had threatened the safety of civilians or damaged civilian property, they would have been unlawful.

A harder determination to make is whether it is unlawful to attack dual-use objects that serve both civilian and military purposes. Cyber attackers may categorize a variety of dual-use objects, such as civilian infrastructure, as legitimate military targets to the extent that they are employed for military purposes. This category includes power-generating stations, telecommunications, and bridges, among other civilian infrastructure used by the military during wartime.

In the realm of cyberspace, most Internet infrastructure can serve as a dual-use object because military systems are so often interwoven with civilian infrastructure. The US military's global communications backbone consists of seven million computing devices on thousands of networks across hundreds of

---

[165] Dancho Danchev, *Coordinated Russia vs. Georgia Cyber Attack in Progress*, ZDNET (Aug. 11, 2008), http://www.zdnet.com/blog/security/coordinated-russia-vs-georgia-cyber attack-in-progress/1670; *Cyber war 2.0: Russia v. Georgia*, DEFENSETECH (Aug. 13, 2008), http://defensetech.org/2008/08/13/cyber-war-2-0-russia-v-georgia/; *Cyber attacks on Georgia Websites Tied to Mob, Russian Government*, LA TIMES (Aug. 13, 2008), http://latimesblogs.latimes.com/technology/2008/08/experts-debate.html; Brian Krebs, *Russian Hacker Forums Fueled Georgia Cyber Attacks*, WASHINGTON POST, (Oct. 16, 2008), http://voices.washingtonpost.com/securityfix/2008/10/report_russian_hacker_forums_f.html; John Markoff, *Before the Gunfire*, NY TIMES (Aug. 12, 2008), http://www.nytimes.com/2008/08/13/technology/13cyber.html?ref=europe

installations in dozens of countries.[166] One study approximates that ninety-five percent of the telecommunications of the Department of Defense travels through the Public Switched Network.[167] Private investment in the underlying infrastructure of the Internet was a key factor in its worldwide spread. Unfortunately, the inter-connected nature of military and civilian infrastructure complicates the lawfulness of cyber attacks by making much of the Internet a dual-use object.

The decision to employ cyber attacks when targeting dual-use objects necessarily hinges on the intent of the attack. A cyber attacker may lawfully target a dual-use object when the purpose of the attack is to gain a military advantage. Contrast this with an attack whose purpose is to demoralize the populace. In the latter case, the attacker is not acting lawfully because the primary object of the attack is not to undermine the military but to undermine civilians' political support for the conflict.

ii.   Are Cyber Attacks Conducted Indiscriminately?

Even if a cyber attack properly distinguishes between a civilian and combatant, a cyber attacker must ensure that its attack operates discriminately to comply with the civilian/combatant distinction. Indiscriminate attacks are those that are so imprecise as to cause collateral damage. Some degree of collateral damage is expected in wartime. After all, war is messy. The

---

[166] William J. Lynn III, *Defending a New Domain: The Pentagon's Cyber Strategy*, FOREIGN AFFAIRS (Sept./Oct. 2010), http://www.foreignaffairs.com/articles/66552/william-j-lynn-iii/defending-a-new-domain.

[167] Jeffrey T.G. Kelsey, Note, Hacking into International Humanitarian Law: The Principles of Distinction and Neutrality in the Age of Cyber Warfare, 106 MICH. L. REV. 1427 (2008).

proportionality requirement is an attempt to limit states from engaging in a foreseeably excessive level of force by requiring states to use lesser methods of force that reduce unnecessary collateral damage when possible.

Article 57 of Additional Protocol I declares that, "when a choice is possible between several military objectives for obtaining a similar military advantage, the objective to be selected shall be the attack on which may be expected to cause the least danger to civilian lives and to civilian objects."[168] Customary law as reflected in Article 57 of the Additional Protocol requires attackers to take "constant care" and "all reasonable precautions" to spare the civilian population and civilian objects. The Additional Protocol, Article 51(4) defines three types of indiscriminate attacks, including attacks that: (1) "are not directed against a specific military objective," (2) "cannot be directed at a specific military objective," and (3) "cannot be limited as required by [international humanitarian law]."[169]

As the definition implies, restraint and control are necessary traits to satisfy the requirement of discrimination. Ideally, cyber weapons would be designed in a manner that permits their operation only against military objects. But this is not always possible. Therefore, the limiting principle is that the more narrowly designed the cyber weapon is to achieve its intended objective, the more likely it is to meet the requirements of discrimination. Importantly, the restraints in international humanitarian law are not meant to be a suicide pact. A state that possesses the ability to design a narrowly tailored cyber weapon is not required to use it if the implementation will endanger its own forces. A state that believes a cyber attack has a thirty percent chance of success in taking down an adversary's

---

[168] Protocol I, *supra* note 46, art. 57(3).

[169] *Id.* art. 51(4).

radar system might choose to engage in a kinetic aerial bombardment with a higher rate of success to avoid risking the lives of their own soldiers.

All things being equal, in many instances, a cyber attack is preferable to a kinetic attack. A cyber attack that takes down an electrical generator will have less physical damage and fewer civilian deaths than a comparable kinetic attack from an aerial bomber. The ability of a cyber attack to disable an adversary's systems without an explosion is inherently more discriminating than a kinetic attack that destroys the same system but also kills the technician operating the system.

But the relative inability of a cyber attack to discriminate raises questions of its lawfulness. Military systems are usually more secure than civilian systems. Therefore, it is easier to unleash a cyber attack that targets a civilian system on which the military relies rather than to attack the military system directly. Further, predicting and understanding the outcome of a cyber attack requires a substantial amount of intelligence on the systems targeted. Even with this information, the number of factors outside of a cyber attacker's control can mean that a cyber attack unintentionally spreads beyond the intended target. Cyber attacks that employ a virus or a worm, for example, can quickly spiral out of control, infiltrating civilian systems and causing damage to property that far surpasses the intent of the cyber attacker.

One example of a cyber attack designed to distinguish between a civilian and a military object with the intent of attacking discriminately is the Stuxnet worm that targeted nuclear facilities in Iran. Stuxnet, a sophisticated computer worm designed to attack industrial control systems, appeared in the cyber ecosystem in 2010.[170] The worm had two main components. One was designed to force Iran's centrifuges to spin out of control. The other was to deceive operators into thinking the machines were operating normally when they were actually tearing themselves apart. The level of sophistication was unprecedented. Not only was Stuxnet designed to upload information about the system it infected to a command-and-control server so that attackers could pick their targets and change how they physically operate, it also appears that it was designed to trigger its payload only for the Iranian nuclear program.

Stuxnet targeted computers known as controllers, which run industrial machinery. These controllers are critical to the successful operation of the uranium enrichment facilities necessary for a nuclear program. The Stuxnet worm became operational when it detected a specific configuration of controllers running a particular set of processes found only in an enrichment plant. While the Stuxnet worm infected civilian industrial control systems around the world, its harmful effect operated directly and exclusively on specific systems and conditions present in Iran's nuclear

---

[170] Robert McMillan, *Stuxnet Worm Hit Industrial Systems*, COMPUTERWORLD (Sept. 14, 2010), http://www.computerworld.com/s/article/print/9185419/Siemens_Stu xnet_worm_hit_industrial_systems?taxonomyName=Network+Secur ity&taxonomyId=142; *Stuxnet Worm Hits Iran Nuclear Plant Staff Computers*, BBC (Sept. 26, 2010), http://www.bbc.co.uk/news/world-middle-east-11414483; Ed Barnes, *Stuxnet Worm Still Out of Control at Iran's Nuclear Sites, Experts Say,* FOX NEWS (Dec. 9, 2010), http://www.foxnews.com/scitech/2010/12/09/despite-iranian-claims-stuxnet-worm-causing-nuclear-havoc/; Christopher Dickey et. al., *The Shadow War*, NEWSWEEK (Dec. 13, 2010), http://www.newsweek.com/2010/12/13/the-covert-war-against-iran-s-nuclear-program.html; Yaakov Katz, *Stuxnet Virus Set Back Iran's Program by 2 Years*, JERUSALEM POST (Dec. 15, 2010), http://www.jpost.com/IranianThreat/News/Article.aspx?id=199475.

program. The Stuxnet worm satisfies the criteria of distinction because the worm was designed for a specific military target—assuming the Natanz plant is not a civilian nuclear energy program—and did not indiscriminately destroy civilian computer systems.[171]

Distinction is a problem for cyber attackers, whose targets are very frequently dual-use. However, if the intent of a cyber attack is to achieve a military advantage by targeting computer systems used for military objectives, and if the attackers conduct such attacks with reasonable precaution for likely collateral effects, cyber weapons are a more precise and adaptable means for attack than traditional weapons.

3.   Proportionality

The principle of proportionality is similar to distinction in that it reflects concern with the consequences of an attack on civilians and civilian objects. Proportionality governs the degree and kind of force used to achieve a military objective by comparing the expected military advantage gained to the expected incidental damage caused to civilians and civilian objects. As one court notes, the laws of war "create[] a delicate balance between two poles: military necessity on one hand, and humanitarian considerations on the other."[172]

The principle of proportionality stems from Article 51 of Additional Protocol I, which states that force is prohibited where it "may be expected to cause incidental loss of civilian life, injury to civilians, damage to civilian objects, or a combination thereof, which

---

[171] Yaakov Katz, *supra* note 171.

[172] HCJ 2056/04 Beit Sourik Village Council v. The Government of Israel [2004], art. 34 (Barak, C.J.),
http://elyon1.court.gov.il/files_eng/04/560/020/A28/04020560.a 28.htm (quoting Dinstein, *Legislative Authority in the Administered Territories*, 2 lyunei Mishpat 505, 509 (1973)).

would be excessive in relation to the concrete and direct military advantage anticipated."[173] Article 57 similarly requires that attackers "refrain from deciding to launch an attack which may be expected to cause incidental . . . [but] excessive [losses] . . . in relation to the concrete and direct military advantage anticipated." The Rome Statute incorporates proportionality within its enumeration of particular crimes. Article 8(2)(a)(iv) references "*extensive destruction* . . . not justified by military necessity" and Article 8(2)(b)(iv) states that "intentionally launching an attack in the knowledge that such attack will cause incidental loss . . . or damage . . . would be clearly *excessive in relation* to the concrete and direct overall military advantage anticipated." In *Beit Sourik*, the court articulated the principle as focusing on "the relationship between the objective whose achievement is being attempted, and the means used to achieve it."[174]

An attack that results in civilian deaths or destruction to civilian property is not a *per se* violation. What is prohibited under the principle of proportionality is an attack that is reckless, or an attack that knowingly takes civilian lives or destroys civilian property in excess of what is necessary for accomplishing a military objective. That is not to say that there is only one appropriate means to achieve an end. Courts have

---

[173] Protocol I, *supra* note 46, art. 51(5).

[174] Beit Sourik, *supra* note 172; *see also* Armed Activities on the Territory of the Congo (Dem. Rep. Congo v. Uganda), 2005 I.C.J. 116, 147 (Dec. 19) ("The Court cannot fail to observe, however, that the taking of airports and towns many hundreds of kilometers from Uganda's border would not seem proportionate to the series of transborder attacks it claimed had given rise to the right of self-defence, not to be necessary to that end.").

recognized that there may be a zone of proportionality within which a commander has discretion to act.[175]

Proportionality applies to the indirect effects of an attack as well. For instance, a cyber attack is responsible for the indirect effects on a civilian population caused by an attack on the control system of an electrical generator. Some attacks have such dangerous indirect effects that they are prohibited outright. As stated in Article 56 of Additional Protocol I, "works or installations containing dangerous forces, namely dams, dykes, and nuclear electrical generating stations, shall not be the object of an attack, even where those objects are military objectives, if such attack may cause the release of dangerous forces and consequent severe losses among the civilian population."

The principle of proportionality ought to make attackers prefer a cyber attack to a kinetic attack. One of the benefits of a cyber attack is that it permits a state to minimize collateral damage. As previously noted, a cyber attack will usually be less deadly than a kinetic attack. Additionally, a cyber attack is potentially reversible. These traits are desirable for a state that wants to apply a level of proportionate force without causing a disproportionate number of civilian casualties.

There are challenges, of course, to whether a cyber attack can meet the necessary requirements to be considered lawful. For example, without a mechanism to reverse an attack, cyber attacks do not allow a target to surrender. Unlike an attack that uses a human operator who can assess changed conditions, a cyber attack that is unleashed into the cyber environment without the ability

---

[175] Beit Sourik, *supra* note 172; *see also* Final Report to the Prosecutor by the Committee Established to Review the NATO Bombing Campaign Against the Federal Republic of Yugoslavia, 50 (2003) (referring to the principle of proportionality in warfare, the committee "suggested that the determination of relative values must be that of the "reasonable military commander").

for recall cannot take into account a targeted state's desire to surrender—a customary right under international law.

As cyber attacks grow increasingly sophisticated, cyber attackers will be able to control them better. For instance, Stuxnet incorporated features designed to limit its effect. Rather than unleash a worm that caused malfunction in all the machines that it infected, Stuxnet operated on a specific target. The destructive effect self-activated only when it encountered the conditions present in that specific target. Stuxnet was also designed to self-destruct when its lifecycle expired in 2012. Features like these better ensure that a cyber attack's effects are limited and proportionate to the military advantage that the attackers hope to gain.

Cyber attackers are not well positioned to refute claims of indirect collateral damage. This presents a problem when a targeted state brings a claim against a cyber attacker. A targeted state has an incentive to exaggerate the effects of force when presenting the attack to its populace and arguing for recourse before the international community. Disproving a state's claim that it experienced inordinate indirect effects from a cyber attack would be difficult. To overcome this problem, the burden of proof should remain with the targeted state. This also reduces the incentive for a state to bring unsubstantiated claims against the cyber attacker. Thus, a state that alleges a war crime would need to bring evidence that a cyber attack was the cause of a disproportionate amount of civilian property damage or death.

The proportionality analysis of a cyber attack must always be considered on a case-by-case basis. A formula that compares the number of civilians killed to the number of combatants killed is insufficient. Rather, one must consider the value of the target and whether the attack offered a definite military advantage and showed proper caution *vis-à-vis* civilian life and property.

4. *Perfidy*

The prohibition on perfidious conduct arises from the desire to restore peace without completely destroying one's adversary. Perfidy is a form of deception, in which one side insists that it is acting in good faith in conducting hostilities but, once an opportunity presents itself, deliberately acts in bad faith. Such unlawful conduct is prohibited under Additional Protocol I, which states that "[a]cts inviting the confidence of an adversary to lead him to believe that he is entitled to, or is obliged to accord, protection under the rules of international law in armed conflict, with intent to betray that confidence, shall constitute perfidy."[176] Perfidious conduct is prohibited under the law of armed conflict because it undermines the ability to restore peace.

One example of prohibited perfidious conduct is if an adversary fires upon armed forces that have already raised the flag of surrender. Raising the flag of surrender carries the implicit promise to lay down arms. Under the prohibition on perfidy, firing in this circumstance is prohibited because using adherence to the law of armed conflict against an enemy is unlawful.

Cyber warfare is enticing for those who wish to indulge in perfidious conduct. Cyber attackers will find bountiful opportunities to influence or mislead adversaries because most sophisticated cyber attacks involve some level of concealment. However, concealment alone does not always present a violation of lawfulness. A *ruse de guerre* is a common tactic of

---

[176] Protocol I, *supra* note 46, art. 37; *see also* Hague IV, *supra* note 149, art. 23(b) ("to kill or wound treacherously individuals belonging to the hostile nation or army" is forbidden).

conventional warfare. Actions such as surprise attacks, feigning attacks or retreats, and psychological tactics are all condoned as lawful efforts to influence or mislead an enemy.

Richard Clarke, Special Advisor to the President on Cybersecurity during the Bush administration, wrote in *Cyber War* of an American cyber attack employed in Iraq.[177] Just before the 2003 US invasion of Iraq, the United States hacked into the Iraqi Defense Ministry's E-mail system. In Clarke's account, the Iraqi military learned that their secret "closed-loop" private military network was compromised when US Central Command (CENTCOM) sent Iraqi military officers an E-mail.[178] CENTCOM stated in the E-mail that the US goal was only to displace Saddam Hussein and his sons from power and they had no interest in harming their forces. The E-mail promised that, if necessary, they would overwhelm any Iraqi opposition as they had done in the Gulf War in the 1990s. Not surprisingly, many Iraqi military officials followed CENTCOM's advice and chose to walk away from the battle before it even began.

CENTCOM's ruse is an example of a legitimate cyber *ruse de guerre*. However, not all cyber attacks will qualify as such. For instance, a cyber attack would violate the law of armed conflict if it sent false information deceiving an adversary's forces into believing that the hostilities are over, inducing them to lay down their arms before a ground attack.

Cyber warfare presents additional complexities in that cyber attacks can deceive targeted states into believing an attack originated from another source, whether the source is a non-combatant or a third party. Under Article 37(1)(c) of the Additional Protocol, "the feigning of civilian, non-combatant status," is an

---

[177] Hague IV, *supra* note 149.
[178] *Id.* art. 23(b).

example of prohibited perfidious conduct. Cyber attackers that trick adversaries into thinking the attack originated from a non-combatant or a civilian violate the laws of war.

But this provision applies only to actions directed against adversaries in armed conflict; thus, an action that tricks third parties to act against adversaries remains a grey area. Such cyber attacks occurred during the Russia-Georgia conflict. There, Russian hacktivists directed their botnets to send a barrage of traffic to the international banking community, pretending to be cyber attacks originating in Georgia. The international banks responded by automatically shutting down access to the Georgian banking sector.[179]

The cyber attack against Georgia reveals the potential for a much larger threat. Had the hacktivists aimed their attacks at another state in tension with Georgia, they could have instigated the opening of another front in Russia's war on Georgia. Such covert action would be perfidious, yet the law of armed conflict falls short of explicitly prohibiting such conduct.

---

[179] Dancho Danchev, *Coordinated Russia vs. Georgia Cyber Attack in Progress*, ZDNET (Aug. 11, 2008), http://www.zdnet.com/blog/security/coordinated-russia-vs-georgia-cyber attack-in-progress/1670; *Cyber war 2.0: Russia v. Georgia*, DEFENSETECH (Aug. 13, 2008), http://defensetech.org/2008/08/13/cyber-war-2-0-russia-v-georgia/; *Cyber attacks on Georgia Websites Tied to Mob, Russian Government*, LA TIMES (Aug. 13, 2008), http://latimesblogs.latimes.com/technology/2008/08/experts-debate.html; Brian Krebs, *Russian Hacker Forums Fueled Georgia Cyber Attacks*, WASHINGTON POST (Oct. 16, 2008), http://voices.washingtonpost.com/securityfix/2008/10/report_russian _hacker_forums_f.html; John Markoff, *Before the Gunfire*, NY TIMES (Aug. 12, 2008), http://www.nytimes.com/2008/08/13/technology/13cyber.html?ref=e urope.

Cyber attackers benefit from the failure of targeted states to detect or attribute cyber attacks. Sophisticated cyber attackers are able to operate in ways that make tracing attacks impossible. This is especially true if tracing an attack requires the cooperation of states with strong domestic privacy laws. The result is that military commanders face less accountability and have more incentives to use cyber weapons.

Perfidious conduct is reprehensible under international law because it punishes adversaries for following the laws of war, so concealing a cyber weapon alone during an armed conflict will not violate the prohibition on perfidy. But a cyber attack that employs an adversary's adherence to international humanitarian law against the adversary is in violation of the prohibition on perfidy.

5. Neutrality

The principle of neutrality permits a state to declare itself neutral to a conflict and thereby protects it from attack or trespass by belligerents. Neutral states remain protected as long as they do not militarily participate or contribute to belligerent states or allow their territory to be used for such militaristic purposes.[180] Notwithstanding these restrictions, a neutral state may maintain its relations with belligerents during hostilities.

The principle of neutrality is derived primarily from the Hague Conventions. The Hague Conventions outline (1) the rights of neutral states and their obligation not to participate in the conflict, and (2) the obligation of belligerents to respect the inviolability of neutral states.[181] Cyber attacks jeopardize these distinct elements of neutrality. The question for cyber attackers is how the

---

[180] Hague Convention (V) Respecting the Rights and Duties of Neutral Powers and Persons in Case of War on Land, U.S.T.S. 540, 2 A.J.I.L. Supp. 117, art. 3, entered into force Jan. 26, 1910.

[181] *Id.* art. 1.

principle of neutrality applies—and whether it is relevant—in the area of cyber warfare.

Under the first clause—the neutral state's obligation—the neutral state is prohibited from participating militarily in a conflict. To retain the title of neutrality, a state may not allow belligerents to move troops, munitions of war, or supplies through neutral territory. If a neutral state permits its territory to be used for these purposes, it loses its veil of neutrality and transforms into a legitimate target.

There is one exception to the inviolability of a neutral state's territory. Under Article 8, a nation need not "forbid or restrict the use on behalf of the belligerents of telegraph or telephone cables or of wireless telegraphy apparatus belonging to it or to companies or private individuals" as long as the neutral states permits the use of its telecommunications infrastructure impartially.[182] Whether this exception applies to Internet infrastructure has not yet been tested.

An element of cyber attacks suggests that this exception should not apply in the domain of cyber warfare. Under the Hague Conventions, belligerents "are forbidden to move troops or convoys of either munitions of war or supplies across the territory of a neutral Power."[183] Cyber attacks operate as weapons. They are capable of causing as much damage and destruction as kinetic weapons. When malware or a DDoS attack is routed through a neutral state, this provision ought to be implicated. If one conceives of cyber weapons as munitions of war, a state's claim of neutrality relies upon whether a cyber attack is transmitted through its Internet infrastructure.

Under the second clause—the belligerent's obligation to the neutral state—the belligerent must

---

[182] Id. art. 8.
[183] Id. art. 2.

respect the inviolability of the neutral state. The perfidious use of cyber weaponry can make this requirement a challenge. A belligerent may not believe a state's claim to neutrality if a cyber attack is designed to appear as if it originated from that state. The danger lies in that a neutral state attacked for this reason may lawfully respond in self-defense, thereby broadening the conflict and violence.

What are the obligations of a neutral state when it comes to cyber warfare? It is unrealistic to require the neutral state to prevent a cyber attack from originating in its territory because of the complex Internet infrastructure involved in perpetrating, as well as preventing, a cyber attack. Cyber battlefields do not exist in a concentrated area. The Internet infrastructure is disparate and extends globally. The method of "distributed communications" developed by Paul Baran and incorporated into the packet switching foundation of the Internet ensures that no user can realistically predict what route information, legitimate or malicious, will take to reach its destination. Information will take whatever is the shortest route to its destination depending upon the real-time conditions at each node. The inability to predict what route malware will take to reach its destination combined with a duty to prevent facilitating an attack would require a neutral state to sever all of its Internet connections in order to remain neutral. Otherwise, a neutral state may unwittingly transmit a cyber attack either directly to the belligerent state or indirectly by routing through another "neutral" state. Such a requirement is impractical.

Neutral states ought to have a way to maintain their neutrality without being held to unrealistic limitations. One commentator suggests viewing the duty of a neutral state through the framework of the law of naval warfare. Under naval warfare, the test to evaluate a neutral party is the "means at its disposal."[184] Thus, a neutral state would need only use the means at its disposal to detect and repel a belligerent's cyber attack within its jurisdiction. Another option is to adopt an intent-based view of neutrality. Under this view, a belligerent does not violate the principle of neutrality unless it intentionally directs cyber weapons through the Internet nodes of a neutral state. Similarly, a neutral state would not be held responsible for unintentionally allowing a cyber-weapon to pass through its jurisdiction. A state put on notice of an ongoing attack ought to cooperate to cease the attacks or else be held complicit.

It is important to maintain the principle of neutrality to prevent warfare from spreading. The infrastructure of the Internet presents practical problems for a state attempting to be neutral under the current international humanitarian law framework. A re-interpretation of neutrality that permits a state to maintain its neutrality despite its cyberspace infrastructure "facilitating" attacks is necessary to preserve the spirit of neutrality. A state ought to be able to maintain its neutrality as long as it upholds its duty "not to allow *knowingly* its territory to be used for acts contrary to the rights of other states."

6.   Unnecessary Suffering

The prohibition against unnecessary suffering restricts a state's arsenal by prohibiting certain types of weapons. International humanitarian law recognizes that "[t]he rights of belligerents to adopt means of injuring the enemy is not unlimited."[185] As noted in an ICJ advisory opinion on nuclear weapons, "states do not have unlimited freedom of choice of means in the

---

[184] Hague Convention (XIII) Concerning the Rights and Duties of Neutral Powers in Naval War, art. 8, entered into force Oct. 18, 1907.
[185] Hague IV, *supra* note 149, at art. 22

weapons they use."[186] The ICJ based its finding on the principle that, "[I]t is prohibited to cause unnecessary suffering to combatants: it is accordingly prohibited to use weapons causing them such harm or uselessly aggravating their suffering."[187]

This prohibition encourages states to use the appropriate level of force to achieve their military ends. The basic idea is that harm should be no greater than is necessary to achieve legitimate military objectives. Under this principle, indiscriminate weapons, such as biological or chemical weapons, are unlawful.

The prohibition on unnecessary suffering cuts both ways in the realm of cyber warfare. On one hand, cyber attacks are often difficult to control, and thus, indiscriminate in their effects. A cyber weapon that employs the use of a worm can unintentionally infect millions of computers in its efforts to act on a single targeted network. Further, a discrete cyber attack can cause unnecessary suffering because it does not arouse suspicion and therefore leads to excessive harm. Consider, for instance, a cyber attack that targets the medical records of an enemy's military commander. If the military commander is given improper treatment that causes unnecessary suffering, the cyber attacker arguably violates the principle against unnecessary suffering. Yet cyber weapons often present the lowest level of force that can be employed when compared with a traditional kinetic attack. A kinetic attack that bombs a building in order to shut down an electrical generator will result in more damage and destruction than a cyber attack targeted at the same electrical generator. Thus, military commanders will often find it preferable to use

---

[186] Legality of the Threat or Use of Nuclear Weapons, Advisory Opinion, 1996 I.C.J. 226, 257 (July 8).

[187] Id.

a cyber attack because it may spare lives and physical infrastructure.

Whether a cyber weapon violates the prohibition on unnecessary suffering is often a case-by-case determination that examines all relevant factors. A good rule of thumb is that a cyber attack is unlawful if its consequences are similar to a kinetic attack that violates the prohibition on unnecessary suffering.

III. CONCLUSION

Cyber attacks are here to stay. Cyber attacks provide a low-cost, remote, instantaneous, and powerful tactic of coercion or destruction, often without triggering accountability. These attributes guarantee that states and non-state actors will continue to develop and unleash cyber attacks in the foreseeable future.

This Article examined to what extent this new form of hostile behavior can be regulated under the existing regime of the laws of war. This Article considered how cyber attacks work, how they are being used in practice, and in what manner international humanitarian law relates to the use of cyber weapons. Without governance—and constraints—from international law, cyberspace will remain a relatively lawless battleground.

Many difficult questions arise when trying to fit cyberspace within a warfare regime constructed long before even the most visionary policy makers imagined cyber weapons. But the problems generated by cyber attacks are often similar to the problems of conventional attacks. The differences between conventional and cyber warfare are of degree, not of kind. Thus, the international humanitarian law regime governing conventional warfare can be effectively transposed to cyber attacks.

Cyber attacks present a litmus test for a nation's commitment to international law. The problem of attribution in cyberspace means that cyber attackers have the capability of coercion on a state without the resultant responsibility. Therefore, the cyber attacker may experience great temptation to violate principles and obligations of international law to achieve the attacker's ends. This threat has generated a substantial amount of interest in rethinking cyber security. While some experts have advocated for less online anonymity and more government control over the cyberspace infrastructure, other solutions exist that create fewer domestic liberty concerns.

The impetus that sparked the innovation of the Internet was the concern of the United States to build a survivable communications system. Today, states experience the same need to create resiliency in their cyberspace infrastructure. Responding to the threat of cyber attacks lies as much in the area of mitigation as it does in the area of attribution. Mitigation means creating systems of redundancy (colloquially known as back-ups) to ensure that systems stay online. Mitigation also means deploying greater intelligence to listen in on chatter of impending cyber attacks so that a state may properly preempt or prepare.

Whatever policies a nation implements to defend its cyberspace infrastructure from attackers, international law must play a role to deter unlawful action by making offenders accountable to international appraisal. An international treaty that regulates the rules of engagement online would certainly be a helpful addition to the corpus of the laws of war. However, in the current international climate, such an addition to the laws of international war is unlikely in the near future. Fortunately, the lack of a cyber-war addendum to the laws of war does not mean that cyber attacks are unregulated. States may continue to rely on the existing regime of international law to regulate cyber attacks,

while they await the international community's response
to this modern form of waging battle.

www.ingramcontent.com/pod-product-compliance
Lightning Source LLC
Chambersburg PA
CBHW072015230526
45468CB00021B/1531